indigoseapress.com

From Victim to Victory

By

Regina K. Lane
and
Dr. Linda F. Felker

Clear Light Books
Published by Indigo Sea Press
Winston-Salem

Clear Light Books
Indigo Sea Press
302 Ricks Drive
Winston-Salem, NC 27103

This book is a work of non-fiction. All ideas, statements, and insights are solely the product of the authors.

Readers should be advised that this book contains a recounting of graphic violence, police procedures, investigations and reports of controversial nature, potentially disturbing photos and descriptions of sensitive cultural and racial events taking place over a twenty-two year time. In their attempt to be accurate and to maintain the integrity of the retelling of these events, the authors have spared no detail. Some readers may find the authenticity of this book challenging or offensive.

All Scripture References are from King James Version of the Holy Bible, and NIV Version of the Holy Bible.

This book is dedicated to Linda E., Kathleen D., Deborah Sykes, and all of the people in the world that have or will have the misfortune of being a victim. We are Survivors! We are all God's children, wonderfully created in His sight.

I am fortunate to find resolution and understanding thanks to the many family and friends who surround me, especially Mark Rabil, Richard McGough, Phoebe Zerwick, Break Thru Films, HBO, SBI, the Winston-Salem Police Department, Sykes Administrative Review Committee, and The Winston-Salem City Council. They never gave up and worked diligently on our cases. THANK YOU!

Many thanks and appreciation to my husband and family, Mrs. Evelyn Jefferson (Deborah Sykes' mother), friends, and acquaintances for their incredible love, support, and prayers, and to God for bringing me to a place I could never have reached on my own.

Although things happen to us that we do not understand, if we trust the Lord Jesus, there are always lessons to learn if we pay close enough attention.

Most of all, I will continue to believe with all my heart that if God brings you to it, He will see you through it. The satisfying part is looking back from where you started and knowing where you are today.

Philippians 4:4-7

Rejoice in the Lord always. Again I say, Rejoice!...The Lord is near. Do not be anxious about anything, but in everything, by prayer and petition, with thanksgiving, present your requests to God. And the peace of God, which transcends all understanding, will guard your hearts and your minds in Christ Jesus.

Hebrews 4:16

Let us therefore come boldly unto the throne of grace, that we may obtain mercy, and find grace to help in time of need.

Psalm 121:8

The Lord shall preserve thy going out and thy coming in from this time forth, and even for evermore.

Preface

In 2012, at the age of 47, as a daughter, wife, mother, stepmother, sister, granddaughter, cousin, aunt, and friend, I would like to proclaim that God has done an incredible thing in my life. I want to tell how He saved me from death with His protective hand. Without Him, I would not be here today. He saved my soul, secured me with His grace, prepared me to survive this horrible ordeal, and brought me forward to this point in my life.

My story is about Amazing Grace. It is about God's love and provision. He healed me. He blessed me. Now, He is allowing me to share with others this story of His awesome power.

My life has never been perfect, but there is comfort in knowing that, even with my faults and mistakes, God still loves me!

I was born in Michigan, and at the very young age of five, I asked Jesus to be my personal Savior. The First Baptist Church of Charlotte, Michigan, played a big part in my early life. My father, mother also joined the church based on their personal experience, and brothers Fred and Tom were saved and baptized.

Readers can visit the First Baptist Church of Charlotte, Michigan on the internet at www.fbcchar.org.

This is when God began preparing me to protect myself, although, of course, I did not realize it at the time. It was a happy time for me as a child, and life was so simple. We lived in a little white house with a big red barn out back. We had animals, pigs, and ponies.

It was there that a pony fell on me, and broke my right arm. I had to learn to do everything left-handed, which I thought was a tremendous inconvenience, even though it was just a part of life. But God's hand was in it, and He was preparing me and strengthening me even then.

My father, Fred Kellar, worked for Owens-Illinois for 34 years, and we moved several times during his career. In the early 1970's, my father was transferred from Michigan to New Jersey.

One day in Bridgeton, New Jersey, I was playing outside with another young girl. We were approached by a 17-year-old teenager, who offered to take us to the store for candy. Tina and I were only eight-years-old, and we thought this was wonderful! People were much friendlier, and not many people in my community even thought about abduction and abuse.

However, Tina's mother and family were very upset about the incident, and called the police to report the teenager's behavior. This was my first interaction with the police department.

An officer came to our home one evening, and questioned me about the incident. I was frightened of speaking with the police, but my mother encouraged me to talk to them. I told the truth, and assured the officer and my parents that I was fine, and that nothing bad happened to us.

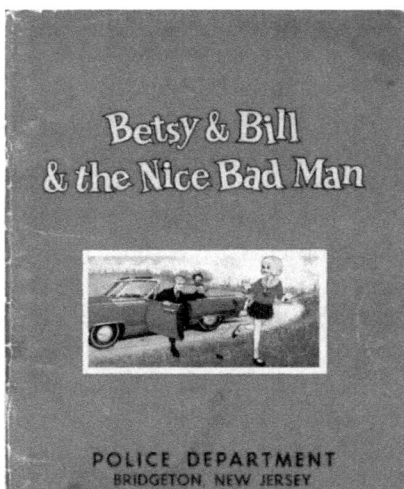

I learned a valuable lesson that day. The officer gave me a book that made a big impression on me. The book, *Betsy, Bill, and the Nice Bad Man,* had a bright blue cover, and told a story similar to my experience. I still have that book today. More than just teaching me a lesson about strangers, it opened my eyes to the dangers that could be around me.

The officer and the book made such an impact on me, that I read it many times and read it to my younger sister. I believed that the police department's primary purpose was to protect and defend the community, including me. I learned to trust and believe in the police.

When I was nine years old, we moved to North Carolina. I continued to grow up in a very normal way, and was involved in many sports activities. Between the ages of 13 and 16, I played softball. Playing softball helped me build strength in my upper body, but especially in my arms. Again, God was preparing me to defend myself. At the time, I thought nothing of this, and was proud to be one of the best left-handed pitchers in our championship league.

I graduated from North Davidson High School in 1982, and yearned to be all grown-up and independent. I moved out of my parents' home and into an apartment with a friend. When I was 18-years-old, I landed a job in downtown Winston-Salem at Integon Insurance Company, which is now GMAC.

I did well in that first job, and at age 19, earned my third promotion into the Commercial Department. Work was busy, and my life was full and happy. I not only had a great job, and an independent lifestyle, but I had also fallen in love with a wonderful man. We made plans to be married, and I believed my future was bright.

Then, tragedy struck our city. In the fall of 1984, Deborah Sykes, a newspaper editor, did not show up for work. I was on my way to the office in my yellow Volkswagen that morning, and I remember the announcer on the radio telling everyone to be careful because a lady was reported missing.

When I arrived at work, I walked to the front side of the Integon Building on 5th Street and looked out. Directly in front of me was the First Baptist Church. I stood there in silence, and prayed for Deborah.

The body of Deborah Sykes was found around 1 p.m. that afternoon in a grassy field, close to where she was abducted earlier that morning. She had been raped, stabbed 16 or 17 times, and murdered only two blocks from my office.

The city was in shock, and police issued warnings for women to use extreme caution until they found and arrested the attacker. The investigation was front-page news, and everyone cooperated and tried to assist the police with solving the crime.

Unknown to the newspaper, there had been two other attacks, one in June 1984 which was two months prior to Deborah's murder. There was another attack on January 1, 1985. Then, on February 2, 1985, something happened that changed my life forever.

This book will detail the events of that day. I am sharing my story not out of a desire for notoriety or fame, and not from any vengeful aspect.

My purpose in telling my story is to exalt the Lord Jesus Christ, and tell of His marvelous grace and mercy to me. I want to tell the world how God prepared me to experience and survive this horrific crime against me, and how He is using my story, and many other stories, to spread the gospel across the world. It is my desire that my story will give people hope, and help them find comfort when something out of their control happens in their life.

God prepared my body to survive a vicious attack. He had a purpose and a plan for my life. I believe that the broken right arm I had as a child, and my involvement in sports activities were all designed by God to strengthen and coordinate my body so that I could fight.

God prepared my mind to survive. He instilled in me a desire to love and serve Him throughout my life. My life was not perfect, God knows there was sin, but at the worst point in the attack on me, God was present in my mind and heart. He was giving me inner strength and a fierce desire to live. He was listening to me, protecting me, supporting me, guiding me, giving me the insight to react.

God prepared the heart of a kind gentleman, Mr. David Wagner, my unsung hero, to intercede on my behalf, and take me, a bleeding and broken stranger, into his home. That man saved me from certain death, and I and my family are forever grateful! My attacker was there, coming after me. God positioned this kind man to be there at the right time, in the right place, and for the right purpose: to save my life.

As I was being attacked that day in 1985, I could not believe that it was happening to me. But, *God was not surprised by what was happening!* He knew, and He was there with me throughout the entire ordeal. Even though I was terrified, in pain, and fighting for my life, God never left me alone.

This book is my personal testimony of God's love. As you read the story, please do not feel sorry for me. Read this story in reverence and honor to our Lord Jesus Christ, and as a tribute to His saving mercy and amazing grace.

Regina K. Lane
February, 2012

Introduction

For years, newspaper articles have stated that "The Integon Victim" refused to press charges against Willard Brown for rape. They never explained why I decided not to press charges. I need to set the record straight, and clearly define the specific reasons why I decided not to press charges against Willard Brown.

A travesty took place; a judgment, with anger, distrust, and blame. The Winston-Salem community heard the stories, shared our concerns for safety, and awaited justice for the guilty. It has taken over twenty years to find more closure.

I will choose to remember Deborah Sykes, Victim #2 as her mother and family have described to me. She was a loving, Christian daughter, who enjoyed singing in her church choir, reaching out to others, the Boy Scouts, and the Jerry Lewis Telethon. To me, she was a very pretty lady with a smile that made you want to smile back. Her life was snatched from her when she had so much to offer and give.

I will choose to remember Linda E, Victim #1, as a woman whose personality was precious and whose voice, full of kindness and beautiful sweetness, seemed to melt away all of the worlds problems.

I am sad that I was unable to meet Kathleen D., Victim # 3, before she passed away in July 2005.

I know from my own personal experience what it feels like to hurt physically, emotionally, deep within my mind, body, and soul. I will not give up in despair, but pray and continue to give it to God. I hope all who read this book will look beyond the hurt in their lives, and set their sights on learning from the past, and living the future to its fullest.

As my wise Pastor, Brother Ed Sears, has said many times to our congregation at Grace Baptist Temple, in Winston-Salem, NC, "Don't let people steal your joy and happiness even though many will try!"

I say "The biggest blessings in life are not received; they

are simply given away with love." I encourage you to seek Christ's love. Your prayers to Him will help you with each step forward in your life. May God bless you and keep you all!

Remember John 3:16: "For God so loved the world that He gave His only begotten son, that whosoever believeth in Him should not perish, but have everlasting life."

Remember Matthew 7:2: "For what judgment ye judge, ye shall be judged: and with what measure ye mete, it shall be measured to you again."

My hope for the community is that, as we open up channels to communicate our stories, learn as much as we can, and try to support one another, that this will be the beginning of the healing process.

Regina K. Lane
February, 2012

Table of Contents

Chapter One: The Attack
~1~

Chapter Two: The Investigation
~13~

Chapter Three: Why I Decided Not to Prosecute
~47~

Chapter Four: 27 Years as the Integon Victim
~67~

Chapter Five: The Big Picture
~79~

Chapter Six: Darryl Hunt Exonerated
~93~

Chapter Seven: Willard Brown's Confession
~107~

Chapter Eight: Sykes Administrative
Review Committee
~119~

Chapter Nine: Why God May Allow Certain Problems
~143~

Chapter Ten: I Have Come By The Way of the Cross
~149~

Epilogue
~153~

Questions
~165~

CHAPTER ONE

The Attack

Psalms 86:1-17 *(*A Prayer of David)
*Hear, O Lord, and answer me, for I am poor and needy.
Guard my life, for I am devoted to you. You are my God;
save your servant who trusts in you. Have mercy on me, O
Lord, abounding in love to all who call to you. Hear my
prayer, O Lord; listen to my cry for mercy. In the day of my
trouble, I will call to you, for you will answer me. The
arrogant are attacking me, O God; a ruthless man seeks my
life – men without regard for you. But you, O Lord, are a
compassionate and gracious God, slow to anger, abounding
in love and faithfulness. Turn to me, and have mercy on me;
Grant me your strength, and save me. Give me a sign of
your goodness, that my enemy may see it and be put to
shame, for you, O Lord, have helped me and comforted me.*

Romans 8:28
*And we know that all things work together for good to them
that love God, to them who are the called according to his
purpose.*

I was a very happy 19-year-old young woman, excited
about my life. After graduating from high school in the
spring of 1982, I moved into a one-bedroom apartment
with a girlfriend. I was thrilled with my newfound
independent lifestyle, and dreamed of one day having a
husband, home, family, and a full rewarding life.

Life was good. I had a wonderful family, and a fantastic

fiancé, who made me laugh a lot and with whom I felt connected. I was also a Christian, with a tremendous faith and trust in the Lord Jesus Christ. I looked forward to an exciting future with the man I loved, and had every expectation of a calm and peaceful life.

I landed a job with a large insurance company in downtown Winston-Salem, NC, and worked hard to establish myself in this position. Very soon, my hard work paid off and I received my first, second, and then my third promotion.

Along with the third promotion came additional responsibility and I was required to work overtime one weekend because the work had fallen behind. I eagerly accepted this, as I could certainly use the extra money for the four hours of work on Saturday. Finances were tight, but I had become quite proficient at maintaining a budget.

It was a gloomy, drizzly day on Saturday morning, February 2, 1985. Most people would have considered staying at home or even sleeping late. I needed four good productive hours at work to catch-up. Therefore off to work I went, arriving between 7:45 and 8 a.m. I parked my yellow Volkswagen in the Integon Insurance Company parking lot on Poplar Street in downtown Winston-Salem, and walked directly across the street to the bottom of the steps leading to the Poplar Street entrance of the building.

As I approached the door, a black male walked up beside me, and I expected him to ask me the time. Instead, he came up and pressed a gun in my side. *"Don't scream. Don't make a move. Let's go back to your car,"* he said, as he grabbed me around the neck and held me tight against his side.

He leaned my head next to his head, and I was leaning into his right side. To any onlookers, it would have appeared that we were a couple. It gave me an eerie feeling.

The man was wearing a grey hooded sweatshirt, with the hood pulled over his head, and a burgundy jacket over the sweatshirt. He repeatedly warned me not to look at him, and it was clear that he did not want me to see his face.

When we reached the car, he opened the passenger door

of my yellow Volkswagen, and told me to get in. Once inside, he instructed me to move over to the driver side of the car, and he sat down in the front passenger seat.

The abductor told me to start the car and drive according to his instructions. He warned me not to do anything that would bring attention to us, and he continued to hold the handgun pressed into my side. I did not want to do anything to accelerate his adrenaline.

Following his instructions, I drove to the intersection of Poplar Street and Fifth Street, and he told me make a right turn. I told him that Fifth Street was a one-way street, so we turned left. I drove left on Broad Street to Spruce Street, and then back again onto Fourth Street. It was like driving through a maze.

As we drove through the middle of downtown Winston-Salem, I noticed that there was a brick wall directly across from the Towne Jewelers building. Briefly, I considered crashing the car into the wall on the other side of the street, but was afraid that someone inside the building might be injured. I was also afraid I would be shot.

The man asked me if I had any kids, and I answered no, but that I hoped to have children one day.

As I drove, I prayed and silently cried out to God. I said, *"Lord, I may not always have lived the way you wanted me to, and I have made many mistakes. However, I ask you right now to help me escape from this attack. I trust you and love you. Give me the strength I need to escape."*

Philippians 4:13 - I can do all things through Christ which strengtheneth me.

I continued to try to look at my abductor, even though he warned me not to. Using much profanity, he repeatedly jabbed the gun at me, telling me not to look at him or he would shoot me. Then, he asked me, *"Do you have any kids?"* It was a chilling question. Why would he ask me about children? I was truly terrified.

I continued driving on Fourth Street, then making turns as instructed, still with the gun pressed into my side. I knew that, at any moment, he could shoot and kill me. I became confused because I was not familiar with the area of town.

I tried valiantly to remain as rational as possible, and knew that in situations like this, it was imperative to stay clear-minded and positive. I took in the surroundings, and was familiar with some of the downtown streets, but only on the far end of downtown where the Integon building was located. I felt like I was in a maze, but wanted to memorize the route we were taking, across railroad tracks, the street signs, Highland Avenue, and other landmarks.

Although it had only been a few minutes since I was kidnapped, it seemed like much longer. I fought the terror that gripped my heart. I cried and pleaded over and over again with the man, hoping to find some spark of compassion and understanding in him. I kept asking him, *"Why are you doing this to me? I haven't done anything to you."*

With each statement, I cautiously glanced over at the man beside me, and he would push the gun deeper into my side and say, *"Don't look at me B--ch. I told you to stop looking at me."*

Pleading and crying, I begged him to release me, but he refused. Finally, he instructed me to stop the car on Old Greensboro Road near the Flamingo Drive-In Theater. It was a wooded, secluded area, and I frantically looked around, searching for some sign of other people that I could signal to help me. There was no one there.

I was terrified, crying, and confused. Who was this black man that abducted me, and was he going to kill me? I cried out of fear and tried to plead with him, begging for my life. *"Why are you doing this to me? I haven't done anything to you, why are you hurting me this way?"*

As he instructed, I pulled the car over in the woods, down a muddy pathway and over a big mound of mud and trash. I told him it was very wet down in the woods, and the car might become stuck in the mud. He told me to drive down there anyway.

When I turned off the ignition, he reached over, grabbed the keys, and threw them onto the floorboard on the passenger's side of the car.

Regina's VW Beetle

As my abductor began to rob me, flashes of my family, especially my baby sister, moved through my mind, like a movie depicting my life. I had heard that this happened just before a person dies. Rebecca, my blond-headed baby sister, was so young and innocent. Thoughts of leaving my Mom, Dad, Fred, Tom, and Patricia, never being able to marry Scott, the man I loved, and dying at 19 years old, were excruciatingly real. I knew I had to survive, for me and for the people I loved. I also knew I was facing a tremendous fight, and I prayed to God for deliverance and protection.

He forced me to hand over my purse, and began ransacking it, dumping everything out. He robbed me of $300, all the cash I had, and threw the change on the floor.

I began to pray in earnest, and approached the Throne of Grace boldly, expecting God to answer me. *Psalms 34:4- I sought the Lord, and he heard me, and delivered me from all my fears.*

It felt like my prayer was transported from the edge of the seashore through space directly into the heavens, and that my mind connected with God's mind, and we were one in prayer.

This was so comforting, and I knew that if it was God's plan for me to leave the world this day, that it was okay. I knew I was in God's hands, and trusted Him to direct the events that were about to happen. Such warmth and peace filled my soul, as God assured me of His presence, and prepared me to fight for my life.

I wanted to be in the center of His will, whatever that might be. Whether I lived or died, I was prepared to accept God's plan. The connection between God's mind and my heart was so strong, that in the midst of this vicious and evil attack, I knew I was His child and that He would be with me until the end.

Meanwhile, there was no reasoning with my attacker. He stated, *"You know what I want B—ch,"* and made me get out of the car, and climb into the back seat.

He saw my watch, and demanded that I give it to him, and I did; however, it hurt my heart to give this watch to him because my Grandmother had bought it for me in Hawaii. However, I took off the watch and handed it to him.

With his gun pointed in my face, he told me to take off my clothes, starting with my blouse, the jeans, and finally my undergarments. I did as he instructed, all the while praying to God to deliver me from this situation.

The black man told me to loosen his belt, which appeared to have a slide clasp similar to a military belt. I refused, and told him I did not know how to unhook that type of belt. He also told me to unzip his pants and he put the gun to my forehead. I was determined not to fully cooperate and calmly submit to the atrocities that were surely about to happen.

My mind raced, trying to think of a way to escape. I thought about using both feet to kick him backwards, but I knew that I would not be able to close the door, grab the keys from the right floorboard, get back in the front seat, and start the car before he broke the window. He would have grabbed me again.

Angrily, he called me a *"stupid B--ch"*, and proceeded to take his pants partially down, exposing himself to me.

He instructed me to turn over, and get on my hands and knees, which I did. He pushed the front passenger seat forward until it touched the front windshield. Then, he told me to lie down on the upturned seat, with my head near the windshield and my legs in the back seat of the car. This was an impossible position to assume, and I was unable to comply.

He flipped the seat up, and tried to rape me by kneeling at the side door of the car; however, his knees would not balance. Then, he climbed into the back seat with me. I braced myself for his attack, all the while praying to God for help.

He forced me to lie on my back on the backseat, and he got into the backseat with me. It was there that he raped me. I prayed for strength and deliverance.

I NEVER EXPECTED NOR DID I WANT TO BE RAPED! Something I said to him made him stop his attack, and he told me to get out of the car. As I stepped out, he demanded that I turn around, bend over, and place both my hands on the roof of the car. With his gun still in his hand, he kicked my legs apart, like an officer making an arrest.

He tried to rape me from behind, but I would not hold still. He was furious that I would not willingly submit to him, and told me if I did not cooperate with his demands, he would "put this somewhere that you don't want it to go." I knew there were only two other openings to my body. I was prodded in the left buttocks, but I refused to submit, moving three more times to stay away from him.

Faced with the evilness of his attack, I believed that the Lord was there with me. I never stopped saying positive, encouraging words to myself, and believed that when I could make my break, I was going to escape and get through this alive or die trying!

Bolstered by these thoughts, my strength was renewed. I knew I would not give up, and would continue to struggle and fight against this vile and horrific assault.

He was unable to rape me outside the car. At that moment, I grabbed his gun from the roof of the car. In anger, I told him that I was going to "blow his black ass off the face of this earth!"

I fired the pistol twice, but it did not discharge. He stopped, and began to pull up his pants, bouncing like a pogo stick. The attacker laughed at me and said, *"Stupid B--ch, it's not loaded, but I have a knife that is going to kill you dead."*

He then pulled out a long butcher knife, and snatched the pistol away from me. As he did, he forcefully struck me with the butt of the pistol on the crown of my head. Another blow to my face, near my left eye, and I thought I would lose consciousness. Feeling my knees wanting to buckle, I knew I could not pass out. I could not go down or he would surely kill me. I knew I had to fight until the end.

I prayed for strength and power, and as I prayed, I remembered that God was with me.

Psalms 22:19 – O my Strength, come quickly to help me.

I had to stay alert now and fight for my life. A tremendous inner strength sprang up within my soul, and I knew it was the presence of God. I fought fiercely to get away, but he grabbed me and came from behind, over my head with a slicing motion with the knife. I caught a glimpse of the blade, and reacted instinctively. Tilting my chin down as he tried to cut my throat, he sliced open my chin instead of my throat.

I wanted to scream but grunted instead, feeling the pain that was inflicted on me. My hand reached up to feel the cut on my face.

He stabbed and slashed me, and I continued to pray to God for miraculous strength to defend myself.

Then, he placed the knife to my throat. I fought hard to keep the knife from cutting me, and grabbed the blade and the handle of the knife with my bare hands. I knew that my fingers could be sewn back on to my hand, but that I would be dead if I released my hold on the knife.

He continued beating my hands and arms with the pistol butt; yet, I never let go of the knife. I remember being slung in a circle, still gripping the knife. My attacker had me pinned down with my bare back on the hood of the car. He was leaning over me, both of us vertically gripping the butcher knife. He was able to once again, slash my face in the chin area. I was holding on for dear life.

We struggled and fought for control of the butcher knife, and fell down a small embankment together. We landed with me laying face down on the ground, and my attacker lying on top of my naked back.

Both of us were still holding the knife, and he was desperately raking his gloved hand through a trash pile looking for anything sharp. With his right hand, he picked up several pieces of broken glass, and slashed away at my face and neck. He raked the shards of glass up across my neck with his grey-gloved hand, but I still would not let go of the knife.

I continued to talk positively to myself, and tell myself that, with God, *all things are possible.* He was my defender and my strength. I reached into the depths of my being, and found the resolve to continue the struggle.

Isaiah 49:29 – He gives strength to the weary and increases the power of the weak.

Using my elbows, and sheer force and strength, I pushed both of us up off the ground and stood face-to-face with my attacker. He was wearing a burgundy jacket, and a sweatshirt underneath it with the hood pulled up over his head. I could only see his face. I observed every detail of his face, his eyes, his nose, and mouth, and I tried to capture his image into my mind.

The fight continued, and I was able to keep the knife away from my throat by extreme determination and force.

With both of us still clinging to the knife, he ordered me to let go. I told him, "No, you're going to kill me," and refused to release my grip on the knife blade or the handle.

Realizing I could now identify him, he increased his demands that I relinquish the knife. "Let go of the knife; let go of the knife," he said.

I told him he was crazy, that I would not let go of the knife so that he could use it to kill me.

I gripped the wooden handle with one hand, and the tip of the blade with the other hand. His hand, with the grey glove, was holding onto the middle of the knife.

9

My hands, arms, and body were beaten and bleeding. He had repeatedly hit me with the butt of the pistol trying to hurt my hands and fingers enough that I would let go of the knife. Nevertheless, I held on.

Confident that he could coerce me into releasing the knife, he told me that, on the count of three, we would together throw the knife away. He did not believe that I could possibly continue to fight him, and that he would regain his hold over me.

He made a swinging motion with his arms as he proposed throwing away the knife, trying to wrestle it away from me. However, with every swing of his arm, I countered with a swinging motion of my own.

He began to count to three, and suddenly, with my every being, I jerked the knife with my left hand, and he lost his balance. His eyes were wide and startled in disbelief as he realized that I had wrestled the knife away from him.

He bowed his back, like a cat on two legs, instinct telling him that I would try to slash him as he had cut me. *I had the knife!*

I turned and started running for my life, and he followed me. I did not look back, but knew he was there, chasing me. With every ounce of remaining energy and strength, I fled out of the woods, naked and barefooted.

He intended to kill me; I had seen his face and could possibly identify him.

As I ran out of the wooded area, I saw a nearby apartment complex. I ran crying toward the nearest house and beat on the door. I did not know if anyone was home.

I saw a curtain move at the window, and a man's face appeared. Just as quickly, the curtain dropped and the man was gone. My heart sank, not knowing if the man inside the house would have the courage to open his door to a naked, bleeding woman holding a large butcher knife!

In a desperate voice, I cried, *"Please help me! Someone is trying to kill me!"*

Then, I heard a sound, and the doorknob jiggled. Then, the door opened slightly. A black man stood there, and he quickly looked to the left and right. Then, he opened the door fully, and pulled me inside to safety.

Once inside, he took a bedspread and wrapped it around my exposed and bleeding body. Leading me to the first bedroom, he left me there long enough to call the police.

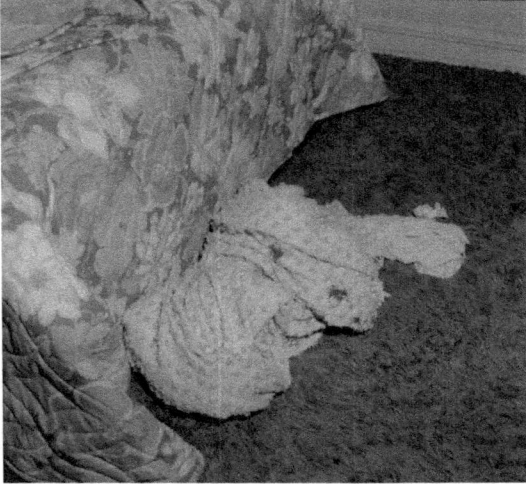

Bedspread wrapped around Regina

I sank to the floor and sat there immobile. I had fought my attacker like a man would fight, and escaped. I was totally drained, my strength was gone, and I was unable to move. I knew I could not fight again.

I had been kidnapped and savagely beaten. I had been robbed of all my money, and even my jewelry. I had been raped and pistol-whipped. I had been stabbed 12 times in the face and neck, with my attacker literally trying to cut my head off with a butcher knife. My body was slashed and bleeding from other injuries and multiple cuts to my upper body.

Yet, PRAISE GOD, *I was alive*. I quietly praised God and thanked Him for delivering me from a certain death. He was my salvation and my strength.

Psalms 46:1 – God is my refuge and strength, an ever-

present help in trouble.

As I sat bleeding on the floor, wrapped in a bedspread, I thanked God for protecting my life, and for providing this kind and gentle stranger to take me into his home.

My attacker had stopped at the edge of the woods when he saw me beating on the door of the house. He waited to see if anyone would have the courage to help me. When he saw the man pull me inside to safety, he turned and fled. I would most surely have died that day if no one had been home or if this stranger had refused to give me shelter.

There was also a fear that swept through my body wondering whether the man opening the door would hurt me, just as he may have feared the same about me.

God miraculously intervened that day to save my life. His power became my power, and His strength, my strength. God's word is true. "I will never leave you nor forsake you." God was faithful, Thank God, I lived.

Exodus 15:2 – The Lord is my strength and salvation. I will praise Him...I will exalt Him.

CHAPTER TWO

The Investigation

Psalms 119:43
Do not snatch the word of truth from my mouth, for I have put my hope in your laws

Imagine the horror, the terror and the shock that my body and mind were suffering at that moment. As I sat there motionless on the floor, wrapped in a bedspread, my energy totally depleted, I knew that it would be impossible to fight my attacker again.

God provided physical strength and inner strength at exactly the right time so that I could withstand the attack, and escape with my life.

As if moving in slow motion, I pulled the bedspread and covered my entire body up to and around my chin. I was reeling from the violence and abuse I had suffered. In shock, I sat quietly and waited for the police and the ambulance to arrive.

I heard the sirens, and knew that the police would be there soon. In my heart, I thanked God for saving my life. Again, my mind went back to that day in my childhood when the police came to speak with me about the teenage boy who offered my friend and me a ride to the candy store.

I took some comfort in knowing that the police would protect me. I trusted them, without having ever met the officers who would be there to assist me and investigate the assault.

13

When the police and ambulance arrived, they rushed into the room where I sat motionless on the floor. As they approached me, I slowly lowered the blood-soaked bedspread from around my face.

Through blurry eyes, I observed the wide-eyed facial expressions of these people as they recoiled and gasped in shock when they saw my bloody face.

Hurriedly, the paramedics viewed my bleeding wounds, and lifted me onto a stretcher. Naked and covered with the bedspread, I had no strength left, and could not lift myself up. The ambulance was there to rush me to Forsyth Memorial Hospital. I was asked if I wanted the siren turned on to get me to the hospital faster. I said "No." I was comforted being with the people who were taking care of me. I started to feel safe in their presence!

Meanwhile, Sgt. Walker had also asked me to describe the man who attacked me. He summoned an Identification Unit to the scene, and ID Officer Pearl answered the call. While I was being transported to the hospital, she took photographs of the bedroom, the crime scene, and the outside door of the apartment.

Mr. Wagner offered his account of the incident, and told the officer how he had let me into the apartment and covered me with a bedspread. Mr. Wagner told the police that I was holding a bloody butcher knife when I arrived, and that the knife was still lying in the hallway.

Officer K. E. Peele seized the butcher knife, which someone had wrapped in a McDonald's bag, and was still in the hallway. The bloody bedspread was also collected.

The investigators located my 1969 yellow Volkswagen in the woods adjacent to the Eastview Apartments.

While their investigation began, the ambulance arrived at Forsyth Memorial Hospital at 9:08 a.m. Could it have only been a little over one hour since my ordeal began? It seemed like much longer; one minute for anyone was too long.

The butcher knife Regina wrestled from her attacker

They rolled me by stretcher into the hospital and placed me in an examination room. This is where I first met Detectives Miller and Barker.

I telephoned my parents, and asked them to come to the hospital. Of course, they rushed to the hospital to be with me. One of the nurses called my fiancé, Scott Lane, who worked for Salem Electric at R. J. Reynolds Whitaker Park, and he immediately came to the hospital. Having my loved ones with me gave me comfort and at last, I began truly felt safe.

Detective Miller asked if I objected to Polaroid pictures being made, and I said, "No." Detective Barker was asked to go to Miller's car and get the camera from behind the seat, and Detective Miller proceeded to take pictures of my wounds.

Afterwards, Dr. Tad Lowdermilk began his examination. Sgt. Walker arrived at the hospital first, followed by Detective Miller to observe my treatment. They continued to ask questions, and an officer took pictures. I knew of Sgt. Walker as I had worked part-time with his niece, Anita, at Sears at Hanes Mall in 1984-85.

15

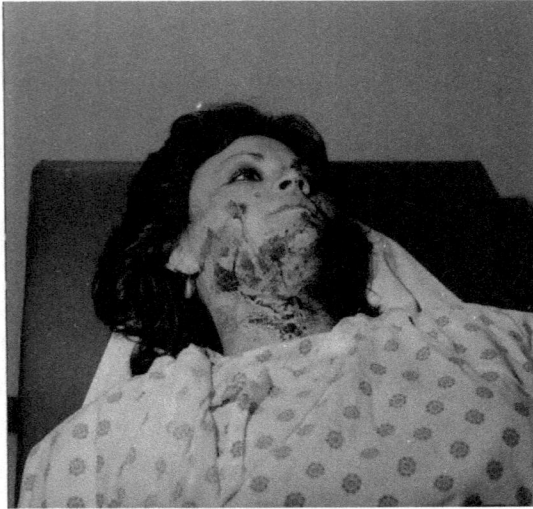

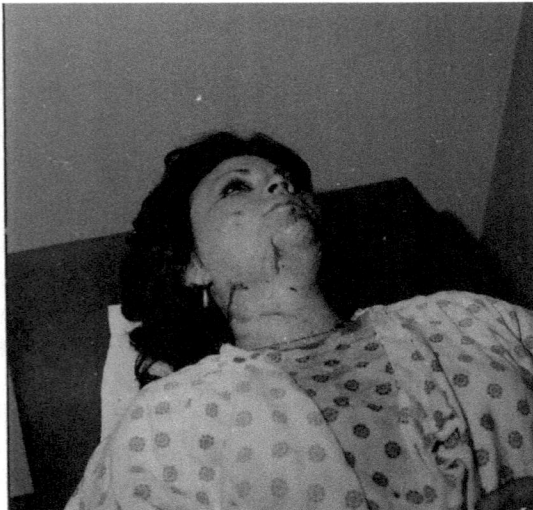

The knife wounds

I was reminded not to pick the dirt out from under my fingernails as it might be needed as evidence. They asked if I scratched or pulled the hair of my attacker, and I said, "No." They told me I should have done this, and I opened my eyes wider in surprise.

For me, this was a living nightmare. Flashbulbs were popping all around my face and body as the police made pictures of me to document the assault, stabbings, and beating I had suffered.

Next was the indignity of submitting to a rape examination. The doctor was extremely kind, and reassured me throughout the entire procedure. The police thought that having the Rape Kit evidence would be essential to prosecuting my attacker. Dr. Tad Lowdermilk performed the rape examination, and confirmed that I had been raped vaginally.

He further stated that he did not find any semen during his examination, and that I told him the rapist did not complete the act. I explained that the rapist was "in once, out once", and how I struggled to prevent him from raping me again from behind.

With the rape examination complete, the doctor continued his examination and began to treat my multiple stab wounds and other injuries. Dr. Lowdermilk cleaned my bloody wounds, face, and hands. He did not just wash away the blood on my whole face. He slowly washed the blood from around the injured areas so more pictures could be made as requested by Detective Miller. My mother was by my side as Dr. Lowdermilk then sutured the cuts and stab wounds. My father, a very gentle man, was pushed to a state of anger knowing someone hurt one of his loved ones, one of his babies.

The police then made more photographs. The police would need "before and after" pictures that completely documented my injuries.

I was released from the hospital at exactly 11:33 a.m. My mind reeled at the events of the morning, and time seemed out-of-perspective. It had only been a few short hours ago that I was in the battle of my life. I kept begging everyone to let me take a shower so I could feel clean again.

During the assault, it seemed that time was frozen. At that moment, I could not possibly have imagined that the nightmare was just beginning and that for the next 22 years, my life would come full circle to the events of that day.

After my release from the hospital, I was taken to the police station. They provided hundreds of photos of black males who were 5' 7" to 5' 9" tall, and asked me to look at each one. They hoped I would be able to identify the man who attacked me earlier that day. I looked at each one carefully, the color of their skin, face, eyes, nose and mouth.

The picture backgrounds varied, making some skin appear darker than others. I wished I had something burgundy like the hood to lay across each picture as I reviewed them. My attacker's chin was mostly covered. This would make identification more difficult.

I thanked God that I was permitted time during the fight to stand face-to-face with the man who was trying to kill me. I had committed his face to memory; I would remember his vicious countenance for the rest of my life.

With my parents present, I began to describe to Detective Miller exactly what had happened to me. I wanted my parents in the room; I needed them to hear and understand what I had been through; I needed their presence and their support. Their love was my anchor of stability as I painstakingly provided every minute detail of the attack and rape.

I spent many long hours that afternoon providing complete and accurate details of my ordeal, beginning with the abduction from the Integon Building.

My attacker had deliberately "leaned" me into him to make it appear that we were a couple. Later, I found out that Detective Miller did not include this piece of information in the official police report, but I felt this was crucial information.

While I was giving my statement, Detective Miller was suddenly called from the room. When he returned, I asked him why he did not write down the specifics of what I had told him about the abduction. Detective Miller told me "those were the kinds of things that would come up if the case ever went to court."

I felt very uncomfortable with this explanation, but tried to reassure myself that the police knew what they were doing and all the information that should be included. Naturally, I wanted a complete report, with every detail intact.

At that time, I began to wonder how accurate the police report would be if the detective could "pick and choose" which parts of my statement would be included in the official police documents.

However, I continued talking, remembering everything I could; but Detective Miller only wrote down the parts he felt were pertinent to the case investigation. While discussing this with Detective Miller, he said something to the effect of, "Well I wrote down that he grabbed your arm; he grabbed your arm, didn't he?" I said, "Yes, he did grab my arm." I know today that Detective Miller did not amend his police report later to include the actual abduction and kidnapping details.

I always felt these details and facts were important. I truly believed that specific kidnapping information would have been another early turning point in my case. People would have read my case and made a comparison to Deborah Sykes case and the way she had been abducted.

Another detail that Detective Miller did not include in the police report was the fact that my attacker threatened to sodomize me. I strongly felt that this was key evidence as to the type of man he was, and the kind of person who would perpetrate this kind of crime. Years later, I still felt there were things that needed to be talked about and clarified.

I was convinced that these details were relevant. My attacker threatened me with sodomy if I did not stop moving when he was trying to rape me outside the car. However, I did not stop moving; I did not want to submit to his vicious assault. I wanted this piece of information fully documented in the police report. Detective Miller did not include those facts in the report. Detective Miller told me that they could not charge my attacker with armed robbery because the gun was not loaded.

Detective Miller wrote portions of the police record on February 5, while I was not present. I later disputed this, and pointed out inconsistencies with what he wrote compared to what I actually said.

The hospital report clearly states that my rape kit was for mobile (moving) sperm from my attacker. The results, none found. This clearly contradicts my police report. I never knew it was not changed.

There was no sex outside the car. Detective Miller said he would change the report later. He never did.

One example of this was concerning the attacker's belt. I told Detective Miller that I refused to remove the man's belt; however, in Detective Miller's report, he states that I did as I was ordered, and removed the belt.

I told Detective Miller that the belt appeared to be a type of military belt, with a slide closure. I took pride in telling him that I refused to remove it, and that I pretended I did not know how to do it. I was forced at gunpoint to unzip my attacker's pants.

As my case was discussed, I was told I should not have left the Integon building at gunpoint. Do not allow other people to tell you that you did something wrong when it comes to trying to save your own life.

Statistics show a better survival rate if the victim is fighting, and not leaving the site where the abduction is taking place. People must do what they feel is needed in order to survive, even if it means going to a secluded area. I prayed, thought about my getaway, and considered what I could do to draw attention to myself.

Victims often feel a degree of satisfaction when they do not comply with everything their attacker tells them to do. This is how I felt, and I wanted that information stated clearly in the police report.

On Day One, I reminded Detective Miller about this error and asked him to set the record straight; however he never made the correction.

The questioning continued, and I described in close detail the man's facial features, and his clothing. I told them about the hooded sweatshirt with the burgundy jacket, and how the man used those garments to shield his identity. I could not see the man's hair or ears.

I tried to remain positive, and my mind took me back to my first encounter with police that evening long ago in

Bridgeton, New Jersey.

Early in my life, I had learned to depend on authority figures for protection and security. I loved my parents. No matter if I was good or bad, Mom and Dad loved me like Christ, with an unconditional love. I respected my teachers and pastor. Growing up, I was taught to respect and trust police officers. I had no reason to doubt them now. I assured myself that they were working in my best interests, and found comfort in those thoughts.

I described having the gun pointed in my face, and being told to take off my blouse, pants, bra, panties, and shoes. There were moments of embarrassment as I included the intimate and personal detail that I was menstruating, and had to remove my feminine protection during the rape. I hoped this would deter the man from raping me, but it did not stop him.

(Interesting that this little piece of testimony was very clearly documented in the police report, but so many facts that I felt were more important were omitted.)

As I told of the rape, I described how he entered me once, and then withdrew. I told of the three times he attempted to enter me again from behind while I was standing outside the car.

I provided explicit examples of the final fight for control of the knife, the multiple stabbings, and how I managed to break free from my attacker.

I was sad to learn first-hand that there were brutal people in the world, without a conscious, that did not care who they hurt, violated, abused, or robbed.

Exhausted, and physically depleted, the interview ended.

My parents later took me home with them to spend the night. I was so relieved to be in their home again, and felt blessed to have family that loved and cared enough to be there with me throughout the day.

That day, and the next day, police officers and investigators examined the crime scene. There was a light drizzle of rain overnight, and the area was still muddy. They took photographs and collected evidence. They found and gathered many blood samples from the car, clothing, trash pile, ground, and surroundings.

They found my car and clothing exactly as I had described to them, and also found and documented the broken bottle glass and other fragments of glass near the trash heap.

The location of the attack

Detective Walker stated in his report that there was evidence of a struggle in front of my car. He also found a bus schedule and a bus transfer ticket, both with blood on them, located on the ground in front of my car.

He found two sets of footprints, one wearing shoes and one without shoes, that led from my car to the edge of the woods. The picture of the shoe prints at the edge of the woods was the only picture I was permitted to see early in the investigation.

Investigators told me that the pictures were too graphic, and that seeing them might upset me. Both sets of shoe prints led down the path toward the apartments. At approximately 75 feet from my car, one set of prints stopped and preceded in another direction, and continued on to Fifth Street. The barefoot set of prints led directly to Mr. David

Wagner's house.

Detective Miller also reported on the footprints, and said that one set of footprints was obviously made by someone wearing tennis shoes and running fast. Investigators were able to create plaster cast footprints and shoeprints.

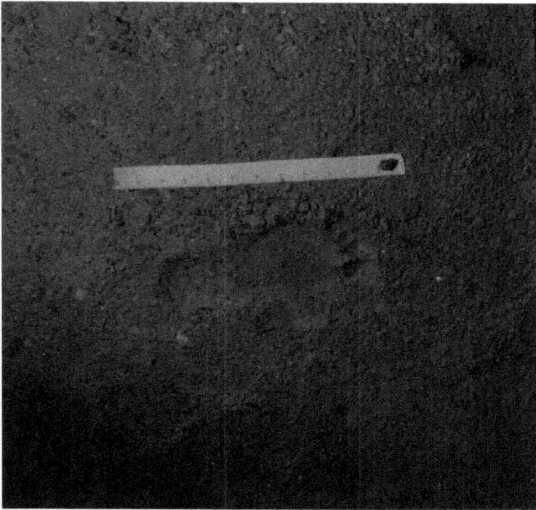

Regina's bare footprint

I was glad they found those shoeprints and felt that it corroborated my story and would help them catch the man who had so savagely attacked and tried to kill me.

In addition, this detailed account of the footprints fully supported my story that the attacker chased me out of the woods, and then watched to see if Mr. Wagner would allow me to come into his house.

It was actually quite easy for investigators to create the plaster casts of the man's footprints because of the rain and mud. He left a perfect trail!

Southside Wrecker Service towed my yellow Volkswagen to the Public Safety Center lot so that officials could process the vehicle for evidence. They also documented the identification numbers of other vehicles that were in the vicinity of the attack. Every other piece of evidence was sealed and taken to the police department.

During their search of the scene of the crime, investigators located the grey glove with bloodstains on East Fifth Street. It was also sealed and retained as evidence.

The attacker's glove

As detectives and investigators combed the neighborhood looking for the criminal, one officer went to visit Mr. David Wagner who had given me refuge in his home. However, Wagner was not in the office when the detectives stopped by to question him.

Later, I was told by Detective Miller, that he went back and talked to Mr. Wagner. Miller told me that Wagner did not see anything, and could add nothing to their investigation.

(It was almost 21 years later that Mr. Wagner told me that the detectives never re-visited him, and never asked him any questions.)

The bloody handprint on Mr. Wagner's door

Mr. Wagner was the only eyewitness of my physical condition the moment that I arrived at his doorstep; yet, he was not questioned and the detectives did not return to his home after their initial evidence-gathering visit.

Detective Miller questioned several residents of Eastview Apartments, and spoke with Mary Louise Cotton, a black woman, who told him that she heard a car outside and looked out her front window. She saw a yellow Volkswagen drive into the wooded area, and said she saw a white female driving the car. Ms. Cotton said that a black male was in the passenger seat of the car, and she estimated that he was in his 20's.

Ms. Cotton said that the black male was wearing something on his head, and she was unable to describe him any further. Ms. Cotton also told the police that residents of the apartment complex had already heard that a black man assaulted a white woman in that area, and that people were anxious about their own safety.

Detective Miller spoke with other residents of the apartment complex after talking with Ms. Cotton, and every person said they did not see or hear anything.

I was still concerned that Detective Miller wrote portions of the official report on February 5, 2005, without my presence. I clarified to Detective Miller that the rape did not occur outside the car, only once inside the car on the backseat.

On February 7, 1985, I worked with a police artist to create a composite artist drawing of the man's face. I had a difficult time. Police tools for a composite drawing at that time were for white men, and my attacker was black. They also wanted me to describe his ears, but the hooded sweatshirt covered them, and I never saw his ears or his whole chin. This was frustrating for me.

The City of Winston-Salem was tense, and people were afraid of further attacks. There was significant pressure on the Police Department, and the public had demanded an arrest for the murder of Deborah Sykes and, now, my attacker.

In order to help secure the safety of people who worked in the downtown area, the composite drawing of my attacker was published in the local newspaper, on local television channels, and given out in person.

Composite drawing of the attacker

In fact, Officer Ingram took the composite drawing to Augsburg Lutheran Church and gave it to the Recreation

Director, Joe Michaelsky. He stated he would make sure all the volunteers were aware of the crime, and show them the composite drawing.

Detective Walker had previously notified security officials at Integon Insurance Corporation where I worked. He informed them that I had been abducted on my way to work. Mr. James Allen, Director of Security at Integon, advised that a video camera installed on the building actually covered the Poplar Street door, and was recording when the abduction took place.

On February 2, Detective Walker asked Mr. Allen to remove the videotape from the camera, and keep it in his custody until the police arrived to take control of it. Detective Miller said that he would personally go to Integon and retrieve the videotape and talk to Mr. Allen.

Detectives Miller, Reaves, and Hicks met with Integon personnel on Monday, February 4, 1985. In attendance were Tom Cobb, the Integon Building Manager, Turner Coley, Vice President of Communications, Bobby Dann, legal department representative, and James Allen, the Director of Security.

The detectives provided the details of the case to the Integon representatives, and found out that there were twenty-one other employees working that Saturday, February 2. However, none of the employees observed or saw anything out of the ordinary while coming from the parking lot to the building.

The Integon representatives were given copies of the composite drawing of the man who kidnapped and raped me, and they said they would post the drawing through the building.

They also distributed copies of the drawing to representatives from Best Western Reservations, which occupied the top floor of the Integon Insurance building.

Both corporate groups asked the police to provide their employees with safety measures and training.

During the meeting, the Integon representatives told the investigators that the video camera located at the entranceway of the Integon Building was not in a position to tape any activities outside the building. The videotape that had been given to the Police Department for review was useless.

This information was a severe blow to me. I was surprised that the camera was not positioned to record the back entrance to the building. It would have been so helpful to my case to have video documentation of my kidnapping.

Disappointed, but not defeated, I continued to provide details of my abduction, and I worked with the investigators to provide them with everything they could possibly need to find the man who tried to kill me.

Detective Barker talked to the Winston-Salem Transit Authority about the bus ticket and bus transfer that they found at the crime scene. He learned that Alvis Reynolds was driving Route 29 on the morning of February 2, and might be able to assist with the investigation.

However, when officials questioned Mr. Reynolds, he said he could not remember the details of any rider meeting the description of the black man who assaulted me.

Miller and Barker spoke with Ms. Gail Taylor, a probation officer at the Hall of Justice. Ms. Taylor told them she was not aware of the recent parole of any sexual offenders in Winston-Salem. They also asked Jim Weakland of the Juvenile Court of the Hall of Justice, but he said he did not know of any juvenile sexual offenders on parole or probation at that time.

Meanwhile, I tried valiantly to maintain my dignity and composure as I again submitted to further questioning and examinations. On February 4, the police made more photographs of my injuries and I continued to answer questions about the assault.

I went with the detectives to the Integon building to show them the exact location of the kidnapping, and pointed out the route I had driven during the abduction.

We drove out of the parking lot on the 400 block of North Poplar Street, and proceeded weaving our way through downtown Winston-Salem. We drove down Fourth Street, Fifth Street, and continued to Old Greensboro Road. Following his directions, we turned east on Old Greensboro

Road, and drove to the Eastview Apartments located in the 2500 block of that street. We turned right, and drove through a muddy pathway, finally arriving at the place in the woods where I was robbed, raped, assaulted, stabbed and beaten.

Traveling this route again so soon after the kidnapping and rape was essential to the investigation, and I was grateful that God allowed me to remember the route.

My mind focused on the horrible attack I had endured in that place, and I thanked my Almighty God and Father for His mercy to me. Without Him, I would not have survived.

Crime Stoppers filmed a re-enactment of the crime on February 9, and broadcast it on area television during the week of February 11, 1985. Many CrimeStoppers reports were received about the case, but there were no investigative leads or possible suspects developed because of the re-enactment.

On February 23, I agreed to ride a city bus along the same bus route that passed in the vicinity of the crime scene. Remembering that a bus ticket was part of the evidence collected on the day of the rape, I wanted to do everything I could to assist the police in solving the crime. I boarded the bus with Detective Miller, followed in a car driven by Captain Cornatzer and Lt. Raker.

The purpose of riding the bus along the same route was to possibly identify and locate a suspect. A black male got on the bus at 7:10 a.m., and was wearing a burgundy jacket.

Police investigators identified him, and asked him to submit to a polygraph test, but he declined. However, I knew he was not the right man, and I could not identify this man as my attacker.

As clearly as possible, I provided the investigators with every word the attacker spoke, the route we drove, and every aspect of the actual attack. I provided a detailed description of the man who kidnapped and raped me.

I described his face in detail, and said that he was dark-skinned with eyes that were slightly set back in his head and that I thought he had short hair underneath the hood that covered his head.

I told them that the man had a slight gap between his two front teeth. I even told the investigators that my abductor had a strong odor of alcohol about him.

I gave them a description of the man's clothing, the blue jeans, a tan belt with a slide buckle similar to an army belt, and a grey hooded sweatshirt. He wore a burgundy jacket over the sweatshirt, and black tennis shoes with white trim. He was also wearing grey gloves.

I vividly described the multiple stabbings, and told how I fought for my life, the struggle for the knife, and an explanation of how I escaped from the rapist.

Early on in the investigation, I called Detective Miller several times a week, if not everyday, to ask if he had any leads in the case. Finally, he told me that I might have to accept the fact that they may not be able to locate and press charges against my attacker.

I went back to work at Integon two weeks after the attack. My friends and I would walk downtown for lunch, and I would scan faces along the way, searching for the man that attacked me. But, I had no luck with these efforts.

The first break in the case happened in May 1985. Detective Crump brought a photo lineup to me, and I made a positive identification of Willard Brown from that photographic lineup. He told me that Detective Miller had brought the picture to him. Brown's family lived two miles from the police department, but it took the police department ten months to find this man.

I reminded Detective Crump that I was still waiting for Willard Brown to be picked up and brought in for questioning.

As the months passed, I went into the police station to review new photographic lineups. I asked about Willard Brown. The answer I received was that the Uniform Division was being sent to find him.

Then, a year later in March 1986, I positively identified Willard Brown in a police lineup. This was an extremely traumatic experience for me.

Brown had been arrested on charges unrelated to my case. Detectives Crumps and Miller escorted me up in an elevator to view the line-up. I told Detective Miller that I thought I would never see him again because of the promotion he received.

Riding the elevator with me was Brown's court-appointed attorney, Ms. Wagner. *(Ironically, I later found out that she was the daughter of Mr. David Wagner who let me into his home the morning of the attack).*

When I was going up on the elevator, I tried to psych myself up, and get ready to possibly face the man that tried to kill me. Knowing that this person was quite capable of murder, I felt a chill run through my body. I was scared.

I was told not to speak with anyone in the lineup, and that someone would speak for me. That was the one thing that I really wanted to do. The man who attacked me had a deep, gruff voice, and I was hoping to hear the voices of the men in the line-up.

Suspect lineup

Not being able to hear their voices my way began to wear away at my confidence. I realized that I should not have gone there alone, but needed the support of my husband and parents.

There was a small window in the elevator, and I was given a paper and pen, and told to write down the number of the person who attacked me. Looking out the window, I could see that there were six men in the line-up. Immediately, I selected number three, Willard Brown.

He stood poised, with his hands behind his back, and he was looking upward and forward with his chin.

Powerful emotions swept through me the moment I saw his face again. Everything poured back on me, and I felt like my knees were buckling; I felt like I was going to drop right there on the elevator.

It was very traumatic for me to look out that elevator window, and see the person that I believed had done those vicious things to me. He had no regard for my life, and would have killed me if God had not given me the strength and will to fight.

I wanted a method to verify the voice, and had previously provided the police with actual quotations of the things that Willard Brown said to me during the attack.

Voice Recognition is as good as a fingerprint as evidence. It seemed a reasonable request to ask for Voice Recognition; however, the police department refused to process my request.

Coincidentally, in the official police reports, it clearly states that the detectives approved the request, and were working to setup the Voice Recognition. The city attorney refused my request. (That is a different response today too!)

I did everything I could possibly do to work with the police department, the detectives, and the investigators to solve this crime.

Each time I met with the police, I asked about the Sykes case, and questioned if the two cases could be related. My case was reassigned from Detective Miller to Detective Crump four days after I was married on May 11, 1985. Detective Crump made a phone call to the Department of Corrections and asked when Brown was in prison. Crump told me that Brown was in prison when Sykes was killed.

I asked for something in writing from the Corrections Department, but was told that I had to believe the information they received. This blew my 100% theory that Deborah's attacker was the same person that attacked me. It put a doubt in my mind that I had identified the right person if he was in-and-out of jail.

I also asked Detective Crump if Willard Brown had any gun or firearm charges on his police record. I wanted to know if he had ever used a gun while committing a crime, or perhaps ever stolen a gun. I was told and shown on his police record that Brown had no gun or firearms incidents on his police record. I discovered years later that this was not true; in fact, Brown's first conviction in 1982 was firearm related.

Continually on my guard, I notified officials every time I saw someone who looked like the suspect. I repeatedly went to the police department to look at photographs, even after I identified Willard Brown, who seemed to live like a chameleon in the town.

I doubted that all the photographs were included in what I was given to me to view.

Yet, the SBI analysis of the evidence was not completed until almost two years later. I was shocked and dismayed as the months went by, and it seemed that nothing was being done to capture Willard Brown. He had been released from jail shortly after I positively identified him in the line-up.

His family only lived a few blocks from the police station, but it took over ten months for his initial arrest. Even then, he was not arrested in connection with my case, but, as we know today, as a suspect in Deborah Sykes homicide.

Interesting that I made the association between my kidnapping and rape and the Deborah Sykes homicide case very early in the investigation, but the detectives and investigators would not listen to me. I was not the only one asking this question.

I asked specific questions as to whether Willard Brown was possibly involved in the Sykes murder, and pointed out similarities between her attack and my attack.

There was never a time that I did not ask Detective Crump about Deborah Sykes case and how things were going. At least three or more times, I asked Detective Miller to change my report to correct the specifics of the abduction, the belt, and the account of the rape. He told me that he would do it later. I also asked him to investigate attempted murder charges. He said, "We'll see."

I specifically told Detective Crump about how I thought the height of an attacker could be different from what an eyewitness sees (my collar was pulled down by my attacker).

I asked Detective Crump if he thought one of the two attackers could have been a smaller build and that maybe he was the one that came back to attack me. I could not get through to them. They did not listen.

My mother-in-law and I talked many times about the two cases. She insulted the police, and talked about how 'crooked' she felt they were. I always came to the defense of the police officials, saying they were not like that. I believe they were honest, integrous, and were doing everything they could do to help me.

I believe it is all in what you are exposed to while growing up. I was not around people who had run-ins with the law, except for occasionally hearing about someone who received a speeding ticket.

I was young, and naïve. My mind could not entertain the possibility that my mother-in-law was right. Again, this goes back to the way I was raised to respect and trust the police. I believed in them, and as a result, did not realize at the time that they were not doing everything they could do to help me.

One week before Darryl Hunt's second trial in 1989, the Winston-Salem Police Department destroyed all of the evidence that was collected by the investigators and detectives to support my case. They offered this to me, but I did not want the terrifying reminder. This included the blood samples, the knife, the grey glove, the bus ticket and transfer, glass, clothes, and the rape kit. There is nothing to analyze. If that evidence were available today, maybe the glove with skin particles inside could be analyzed using current DNA testing.

Although they still have the 'before and after' pictures,

and photographs of the footprints and crime scene, the physical evidence is gone.

What would have happened if I had kept the evidence box and opened it? They might say that, because the evidence was tampered with, it was therefore contaminated and would not hold up in court as credible evidence.

Chronology of Police Reports

DATE OF REPORT	TYPE OF REPORT	CONTENTS OF REPORT	WRITER OF REPORT
2/2/85	Complaint Report	Initial Police Report documenting the kidnapping, rape, armed robbery, beating, and stabbing of Regina F. Kellar.	Peele
2/2/85	Supplement Report	The search of the crime scene and the evidence collection.	White
2/2/85	Supplement Report	Collection of photographic evidence from the Eastview Apts. And the crime scene.	Vickie Pearl
2/2/85	Composite Drawing and Wanted Poster	Creation of a composite drawing of the suspect. Wanted poster sent to appropriate units and divisions. Kellar shown photographs of black males under 34 years old, but did not identify a suspect.	K. R. Hutchens

2/2/85	Supplement Report	Photographs of Kellar at hospital, photographs from the crime scene, and two plaster impressions of foot/shoe prints.	K. F. Schulte
2/2/85	Request for Examination of Physical Evidence	All physical evidence sent to the SBI in Raleigh, NC. Plaster impressions of foot and shoe prints sent to SBI for examination and analysis.	Sgt. W. L. Brindle
2/5/85	Supplement Report	Detective. Miller's official Report that documents the initial investigation and interrogation of Kellar on 2/2/85 and describes her physical injuries. Composite drawing by K. R. Hutchen provided to Lt. Tise of the Patrol Division for circulation.	Det. W. G. Miller
2/5/85	Supplement Report (cont)	Kellar identified butcher knife and grey glove. Det. Barker met with personnel at WS Mass Transit Authority and	Det. W. G. Miller

		questioned the bus driver. Details of meeting with Integon personnel on 2/4/85. Kellar retraced route from the Integon Bldg. to the scene of the crime.	
2/5/85	Supplement Report (cont)	Integon personnel tell the Police that the video camera at the entrance of the Integon Building was not in a position to tape or record any activities outside the door.	Det. W. G. Miller
2/6/85	Supplement Report	The report, written on 2/6, describes events of 2/2/85. Plaster casts of both right and left shoe prints made, and Residents of the Eastview Apartments were interviewed.	Det. W. G. Miller
2/26/85	SBI	Rape kit submitted to SBI	
2/27/85	Supplement Report	Kellar and Miller rode city bus through downtown Winston-Salem searching for suspects that met the description.	Det. W. G. Miller

		Negative results.	
2/27/85	Supplement Report	Miller requests polygraph of Carl Graham. Graham declines.	Miller
3/4/85	Supplement Report	Police interrogation of Billy Thompson on 2/7/85.	Miller
3/4/85	Supplement Report	Crimestoppers film made on 2/9/85; shown on area television the week of 2/11/85. Details of Kellar and Miller bus ride on 2/23/85 looking for a suspect meeting attacker description	Miller
3/20/85	Laboratory Report	Results of physical lab evidence received. (*Cannot locate these results today*). Miller informed Kellar there was no match on blood samples, and that there are no DNA tests to compare texture of hair, glove to suspect.	SBI
3/21/85	Supplement Report	Kellar and Miller ride bus route to locate possible suspect. Kellar	Miller

		states Carl Graham is not the man who raped her.	
4/22/85	Supplement Report	SBI had not examined plaster casts.	Miller
5/15/85	Supplement Report	Case reassigned to Det. W. C. Crump	Crump
5/28/85	Supplement Report	Kellar married; new name is Lane. Lane identifies Willard Brown during a photographic lineup on 5/25/85.	Crump
6/3/85	Supplement Report	SBI Lab Report on plaster casts received. SBI Lab Report on physical evidence. Search continues for Willard Brown	Crump
6/17/85	Supplement Report	6/13/85 – Lane observes suspect in Integon area. Suspect not located.	Crump
6/17/85	Supplement Report	6/15/85 – Lane contacts Crump and advises the suspect was a witness in the Darryl Hunt trial. Crump advises he will be on vacation thru 6/24/85	Crump
6/27/85	Supplement	Details of three	Crump

	Report	photo lineups shown to Lane. Willard Brown identified in 3rd lineup. Two outstanding unrelated warrants for Brown.	
7/12/85	Supplement Report	7/1/85, Lane advises Willard Brown in downtown area. As of 7/10/85, unable to locate Willard Brown.	Crump
7/19/85	Supplement Report	7/17/85 Lane requests to view IDMO photographic file. She reviewed 350 photos. Lane advised police that suspect had a black gun.	Crump
7/19/85	Supplement Report	Unable to locate Willard Brown.	Crump
8/6/85	Supplement Report	Unable to locate Willard Brown	Crump
8/15/85	Supplement Report	Lane observed suspect in downtown area. Unable to locate suspect.	L. D. Sanders
8/15/85	Supplement Report	Lane and police artist create composite drawing and wanted poster of suspect.	M. T. Rumple

9/12/85	Supplement Report	Due to other job assignments, Crump unable to contact Lane for interview. Requested Det. Johnson to video tape areas of downtown the week of 9/2 and 9/6/85.	
10/3/85	Supplement Report	No new leads.	Crump
10/24/85	Supplement Report	Unable to locate Willard Brown.	Crump
11/14/85	Supplement Report	Unable to locate Willard Brown	Crump
12/24/85	Supplement Report	Unable to locate Willard Brown	Crump
1/23/85	Supplement Report	Unable to locate Willard Brown	Crump
1/27/86	SBI Lab Report	Lab report analysis and evidence returned to Police Department by SBI	
2/3/86	Supplement Report	Unable to locate Willard Brown. Crump advises Lane that the case will be Closed – Inactive	Crump
2/23/86	Supplement Report	Case re-opened. Lane views new photo lineup with negative results.	Crump
3/10/86	Supplement Report	Lane views photo lineup with	Crump

		negative results. The Case was again Closed – Inactive.	
3/18/86	Sykes Homicide Report	Willard Brown arrested as possible suspect in Sykes homicide.	Crump
4/1/86	Supplement Report	Photos made of Willard Brown and other subjects	L. R. Frye
4/25/86	Supplement Report	Lane identifies Willard Brown in on-view lineup. Physical evidence collected via search warrant of suspect. Evidence sent to SBI Lab.	Crump
5/14/86	Supplement Report	Lab results not yet received from SBI	Crump
5/14/86	SBI	Lab Results submitted	
6/10/86	Supplement Report	5/20/85 Lane requested voice analysis of Willard Brown. Crump advised Lane to write quotes of the suspect. Crump states he will make a recording of quotations from Lane's list and have suspect report those quotes in a Voice Identification	Crump

		Line-Up.	
7/8/86	Supplement Report	Willard Brown in Alexander Prison Unit on earlier conviction. Police Legal Advisor, Claire McNaught, advised Crump not to use vocal identification. No lab results received as of 7/2/86.	
8/28/86	Supplement Report	SBI analysis of evidence has not been completed.	Crump
10/15/86	Supplement Report	Crump called SBI Lab. SBI analysis of evidence has not been completed.	Crump
11/10/86	Supplement Report	SBI analysis of evidence has not been completed.	Crump
12/3/86	Supplement Report	SBI analysis of evidence has not been completed. Chemist on leave.	Crump
12/22/86	Supplement Report	SBI analysis of evidence has not been completed.	Crump
1/23/87	Supplement Report	SBI analysis of evidence has not been completed.	Crump
02/12/87	Supplement Report	Crump went to Wilkes Cty. Prison to interview Willard Brown, who	Crump

		requested an attorney. Crump left without asking Brown any questions other than who might serve as an alibi for activities on 2/2/85.	
3/12/87	Supplement Report	Attempt to interview Brown's mother with negative results	Crump
4/1/87	Supplement Report	Attempt to contact Brown's mother, negative results	Crump
4/10/87	Supplement Report	Interview with Brown's mother. Brown living in High Point with girlfriend.	Crump
5/5/87	Supplement Report	On 4/15/87, attempt to locate Brown's alibi witnesses with negative results.	Crump
5/5/87	Supplement Report	4/30/87. Crump asks Lane if she wants to prosecute based solely on her identification of Brown; no other evidence. Lane declines. Case is Closed – Exceptionally Cleared.	Crump
9/10/89	Supplement Report	Case Closed – Exceptionally	Crump

		Cleared. Lane identified Willard Brown as her attacker and does not wish to prosecute.	
1989	NOTE	All evidence destroyed by Winston-Salem Police Department	

CHAPTER THREE

Why I Decided Not to Prosecute Willard Brown

Isaiah 59:14
So justice is driven back, and righteousness stands at a distance; truth has stumbled in the streets, honesty cannot enter.

I wanted and deserved justice for what he had done to me. However, when it came down to pressing charges against Willard Brown, I found out that I was wrong to put my trust in some people in the Winston-Salem Police Department to help me solve this crime.

I was not only faced with making the decision on whether to press charges against Brown, but also having to determine if the police had enough evidence to gain an actual conviction of Willard Brown.

From the beginning of the investigation, I asked the right questions, and did everything I could to assist the detectives in the investigation. I cooperated fully with the police, and provided them with every detail of information. And, from the beginning of the investigation, I asked repeatedly if my attacker could be the same person who raped and murdered Deborah Sykes.

The first time I asked this question was just a few days after my attack, while I was helping the artist complete a composite drawing of Willard Brown.

I specifically asked Detective Mike Barker if the same

person that attacked me could be the one that got Deborah Sykes. I asked Detective Barker if the information from my case had been compared to the information in the Sykes case.

Detective Barker said he did not know, and deferred the question to Detective Bill Miller. After walking away again, and returning, Miller said in a very firm voice, "They already have the one that raped and killed Deborah Sykes in jail. They do not want to do anything that would make people ask questions or put doubts in people's mind because it could hurt their case."

Detective Miller told me that, even though there was a knife, there were no other similarities. I thought there were many similarities, including the fact that we were both white women, abducted in the early morning, raped in secluded areas, and stabbed with a knife.

Miller assured me that according to two eyewitness accounts, Deborah Sykes' attackers were big men, over six feel tall. My attacker was not that tall, so Detective Miller concluded that I was wrong.

The eyewitness accounts are different because I was grabbed around the neck and pulled into my attacker. A victim would look shorter if the attacker was taller. Immediately, I was shown pictures of Darryl Hunt and Sammy Mitchell. I knew they did not hurt me.

I was not satisfied with Detective Miller's answer, and could not understand why they refused to compare the evidence between the two cases, but they were in charge. Wasn't the whole purpose of an investigation to find out the truth?

During the investigation, I cooperated fully, did everything they ask me to do, and initiated many contacts with the police trying to help them locate and arrest Willard Brown.

They finally arrested him on charges that were not even related to my case, but as a suspect in the Deborah Sykes murder! How was that possible? I asked the question over and over if my attacker could be the same one that killed Sykes, and was told it was not possible.

One year later, they arrested him on suspicion of murdering Deborah Sykes. However, even then, they did not do a comparison of the evidence from my case to the Sykes case. If they had, perhaps the blood sample match would have solved my case and Deborah's case.

When it came down to pressing charges against Willard Brown, I was faced with many obstacles, barriers, and lack of support from the Winston-Salem Police Department in supporting the charges and providing evidence.

I asked again if Brown could have also been the person that raped and murdered Deborah Sykes. Detective Crump told me no, that Brown was in prison at the time of the Sykes murder.

We now know that Willard Brown was not in prison. I was given incorrect information and I based my decision partly on this.

I asked the question, did Willard Brown ever own, ever steal or ever have possession of a gun. I was told they did not know, and there was no police record of it.

Again, I received bad information from the police department. I was severely misled, and this bad information contributed significantly to my decision.

One of the saddest things for me was when I worked with Lt. Joseph Ferrelli. He encouraged me to go to the Department of Corrections website and review Willard Brown's criminal record. Phoebe Zerwick, a reporter with the Winston-Salem Journal, did a thorough job of investigating and also provided this information.

She, along with Lt. Ferrelli, provided me with the complete police record for Willard Brown. I saw the report from 1982; there was a gun charge. I asked Detective Crump this question many times. It might have changed my decision on whether to press charges against Brown if I had been able to have the complete report.

The police did not fully disclose Brown's record. They gave me wrong information about the date of Willard Brown's release from jail. They told me he did not have a firearm conviction. The firearm conviction is actually the first conviction on his record from 1982 on his police record. The release date needs to be changed on the Department of Corrections website.

Years later, looking through Willard Brown's police record, I saw convictions from 1982 for firearm possession. Moving forward through the report, he had charges and convictions for a multitude of other crimes, including murder, drugs, theft, trespassing, vehicle offender, possession and common law robbery.

If the police had not been so focused on Darryl Hunt and Sammy Mitchell, this crime against me may not have been committed.

I was told Willard Brown, his girlfriend Frieda and two other people lived in High Point. The truth is Frieda lived in the Maryland Avenue Apartments, only a few short blocks from where Willard Brown raped me.

Sergeant Chuck Bryom, a man of compassion, was kind enough to drive me back to those apartments on November 7, 2006. He showed me where Frieda lived. He showed me the hill Willard Brown would have run down when making his escape from the crime scene.

Police photos document Willard Brown's escape and footprints. I jokingly said I guess it would have taken two minutes for him to run. Sergeant Bryom said, *"No, one minute, throwing the bloody glove on Fifth Street, and then running to the apartment."*

My case was mishandled from the start. There were inappropriate things said to me that undermined my confidence and made me feel like the perpetrator rather the victim.

In fact, Detective Miller made me feel like what happened to me was partly my fault. He insinuated that I cooperated with Brown. Then, he told me he had to make sure I did not do these things to myself. I was devastated that he would think I could possibly be responsible for kidnapping, raping, robbing, and stabbing myself! No wonder I felt intimidated about pressing charges against Willard Brown.

Was it that he did not believe me? There I stood, with over 30 stitches in my head and my face, not counting the cuts to my neck and hands. I had been kidnapped at gunpoint, pistol-whipped in the head, down the left eye, raped, and beaten. Not to even mention having to run from the woods, exposed and weak from fighting for my life, completely naked in my 125-pound body, not knowing if help would be waiting at the door. I knew I had escaped my attacker; my body was shaking as though someone had dropped me into cold ice water.

I was tremendously upset by his comment. Seeing how distraught I was, Miller said, *"I'm sorry. You would be amazed at how many people accuse others of rape and then we find out that it was consensual."*

How could I possibly ever expect justice when the lead detective makes such an incredulous statement!

Detective Miller implied and even wondered if I had perpetrated these horrendous acts on myself.

I remember thinking to myself how Miller could possibly even think that I would consent to any of these brutal acts. It appeared that Miller was trying to discredit me as a witness, and the validity of the entire case. Maybe he wanted to see my reaction of whether I would be upset or not. Yes, in the backseat of the detective's car, I thought I was going to cry.

I was 19 years old. It seemed to me like the officials were working against me rather than for me. I had to dispute with the lead detective over inconsistencies in the official police report, and was faced with him refusing to make the corrections.

On the morning after my attack, a reporter for the Winston-Salem Journal asked to speak with me about my experience. I declined the interview because the reporter told me they would use my name in the newspaper. When I told Detective Miller about the request, he told me that it was a good thing I did not talk to the reporter because she was gay.

I was shocked! I did not care about the reporter's sexual preferences; I just wanted to find the man that tried to kill me.

In February 2006 when I first addressed the Sykes

Administrative Review Committee and shared this information, Lee Garrity, our current 2006 City Manager, mouth dropped open. I read his lips as he said to himself, "That should never have happened." I was glad to see he was an expressive person.

I felt neglected during the investigation of my kidnapping, rape, and attempted murder. The detectives implied that I was not a priority. This assumption is supported in their various supplemental police reports. Time after time the writers of these reports state that their workload was too heavy to spend any time on my case.

I had married, and moved; however, the police could have contacted me at any time at Integon. I did not change employers, and was always available to help them in the investigation. They always knew where to find me.

Time after time the monthly supplemental reports state that they cannot locate Willard Brown. Yet, the reports provide little if no details on any actual efforts to find Brown. What were they doing to find him? There is no indication that anything was being done to help me through any of these reports. I was always told the Uniform Division was searching for Willard Brown.

No one was listening to me. I believed there was a connection between my case and the Sykes case, and the police could not help me prove that in 1985–1986. I was told that they had already arrested Darryl Hunt, and did not want to do anything to jeopardize their case against him.

The police never made a cross-examination of the evidence between my case and Deborah Sykes case. We know today that they refused to parallel the evidence for fear it would damage their pending case against Darryl Hunt.

I was told in 1985 that the investigators did not want to ask any questions that would put doubt in people's minds, and hurt the case against the man they had in jail for the murder of Deborah Sykes. That was Detective Miller's actual statement to me whenever I asked about any possible connection between the two cases.

There were many similarities between my case and the Sykes case, but they refused to even consider the possibility that they had arrested the wrong man.

During my investigation by Detective Miller, I asked him if there had been any other attacks like mine. Miller told me that he was not aware of any other rape cases, but that other detectives might be working on things he did not know about.

We know today, that there was a weekly meeting that included all investigators and detectives. At this meeting, they shared updates of all cases they were working on, and compared notes. Detective Miller obviously knew about the other rapes and assaults in the area.

The police told me that they could not help me prove my case. I thought that proving my case was their job, not mine. I mistakenly believed that the detectives and investigators primary role was to uncover the truth and find evidence to support the truth. But, they were not interested in finding the truth or the evidence, or sharing information about the past abductions that occurred around that time.

The police were dealing with public pressure over the Sykes/Hunt case. It was not only public pressure, but political pressure. An extreme amount of cover-up was taking place, and I was victimized yet again, through the handling of my case.

Anytime police officers have to deal with the press, it creates additional pressure for them. However, looking back, it is evident that the press was actually trying to help the police solve my case. They were investigating and providing detailed information that was being overlooked by investigators and detectives.

I chose not to participate in Darryl's case because I knew it needed to be worked out between the police and Darryl's defense team. I knew Darryl had done nothing to me. I did not want to do or say anything that would jeopardize progress and Darryl's release from prison.

I was upset that the police could not help me prove my case. I gave the detectives the details of the abduction from the building. I tried to ask the right questions on February 7, 1985 including, could Brown be the same person who attacked Sykes. I talked to my parents, Fred and Sandy

Kellar, and Mary Lane, my Mother-in-Law, about this many times. I wondered if Willard Brown had the capability to do that. My attack was six months after Deborah's attack, and the incidents, as we know today, are very similar.

I have found a great friend in Richard since January 12, 2004. I had many conversations with Richard McGough, Darryl Hunt's 1990's investigator, but I was respectful of the police and waited to be asked to discuss my case with the police.

I needed to be in control of how my information would be released. I did not want to hurt the Sykes family, or create any problems that might hinder Darryl's release.

My first phone messages from Mark Rabil were on January 17, 2004. I returned the call to Mark on January 19, 2004, and we spoke for 30 minutes. One of the most astounding things he said to me was "If I had prosecuted Willard Brown, Darryl Hunt could possibly be in jail today." I had tried on two different occasions to meet with Tom Keith, Mark Rabil, and the police; however, it was never permitted. Mark and Richard waited two years to speak with me.

I spoke to the Sykes Administrative Review Committee on February 2, 2006. I had invited Mark and Richard to attend; they were hearing this information for the first time.

On February 19, 2006, when I explained to Mark and Richard the details about my abduction, they stopped writing, looked up, looked at each other, and then looked at my mother and me. They said, "Just like the eyewitness accounts of seeing Deborah that morning." Deborah's attack occurred in the same vicinity; she was raped, sodomized, stabbed, and murdered. The primary difference between her case and mine is that Brown was unable to sodomize me (although he tried three times), and I escaped after a horrendous fight for my life. Why didn't the police make the comparison?

Another disheartening fact back then was that Detective Miller's report of my attack had so many wrong facts. He told me he would make corrections to the report; he said he would do it later. He was determined to leave everything in the report the exact way he had written it, even though it was not completely accurate. Or, he was too busy or maybe even forgot to make the corrections.

Another example of questionable information that I received from the detectives was about the armed robbery charges. Detective Miller told me it was not armed robbery because the gun was not loaded. And there is the example of the actual rape. I told it, detail by detail, exactly the way it happened to me. I described having the gun pointed in my face, and being told to remove each article of clothing in sequence. I told Miller that I refused to unlatch Brown's belt. However, Miller's report states that I "did as I was ordered."

The police seemed defeated, even after the first couple of hours. Detective Miller and my Dad were in the crime lab and walked around the car. Miller told my Dad, "We'll probably never catch this guy that hurt your daughter." My account today is the way my family also remembers.

Another detail of the rape that was not disclosed in the police report was the fact that I said, "The attacker went in me once and right back out." This was not disclosed. Although it was still a rape, the report makes it appear that the act was concluded, and that another rape continued to take place outside the car.

I refused to submit to the rape and made it too difficult for Brown to continue his assault. I refused to stop moving. I tried to get Detective Miller to change that part of the report, but he did not. He said he was trying to help me along (as he wrote the February 5, 1985 report in my absence) and as recorded in Chief Masten's letter in a Winston-Salem Journal article.

I knew it was awkward to address everything that would have any possible bearing on my case. I argued with Detective Miller about the way he wrote the report. I wanted him to include all the facts about the case, and that I did not voluntarily submit to the attack.

Two weeks after the attack, I returned to work at Integon. Detective Miller and I met with the James Allen, the Head of Security, prior to my return because I was concerned about my safety. That day, I asked Detective Miller if the charge of attempted murder could be added to the record, and explained tucking my head against my chest, which stopped Brown from slicing my throat, and not just once. Instead, he cut my chin. My attacker had every intention of killing me.

Miller's response was, "We'll see." The charge was never added.

I knew there were no fingerprints on the knife because my attacker was wearing grey gloves when he stabbed me. I asked about any hair that might have been found inside the glove, and I asked about testing for that particular aspect. I was told that if hair was found in the glove, it would be hard to make a comparison. I also thought I had cut Brown's hand when I jerked the knife away from him.

Detective Miller told me that it would be hard to make a comparison of these things. The glove was not analyzed for skin particles, or other things that could be used in court.

I wanted investigators to compare the shoe size prints at the crime scene to Willard Brown's foot size. They did not feel it was significant. The prints were not compared. Another comparison was whether he was right-handed. He leaned me into his right side when I was abducted from the building, and the shards of glass from the trash heap that he raked across my neck were from left to right.

It was raining the day of the attack. My fiancé, Scott Lane, was upset because the investigators refused to bring out trained dogs to track the scent of my attacker. The police said the reason they did not use this method of search was because it was raining.

They had the glove and knew which direction the footprints led down the embankment, and possibly to the apartments across the street. We would have been so close to catching him if the Police had used the dogs to track my attacker.

Years later, during the investigation with the Sykes Administrative Review Committee, I found out that this explanation was not true. Lt. Joseph Ferrelli told Mark Rabil and me when we went to the Police Department to view pictures of my crime scene that, according to experts who work with K9's, the best time to use tracking dogs is when it is raining. Dogs' noses are actually very moist and they are able to track well in the rain.

There were several things I tried to explain to Detective Miller, and others, throughout the years. Miller did not add all the details of my case when he wrote the original police report. If he had, there would have been more of an immediate comparison between Deborah's death and my attack.

My other question, 'were there other attacks', could have been very successful in resolving this situation earlier on for all of us.

I told Detective Miller and Detective Crump several times, how the height of an attacker could be different from what someone would be able to perceive, based on the abduction.

Detective Miller never documented the manner in which I was abducted away from the Integon building. In fact, while I was giving my first statement, with my parents present, we were interrupted, and Detective Miller got up and left the room.

When he came back, I specifically asked Detective Miller why he did not write down the abduction from the building. I said, "Why didn't you write down that he grabbed me around the collar and leaned me into him like we were together? If someone saw us, they would have thought we were together."

I later learned that these same things were testified to in court during the Sykes trial. Eyewitnesses said that the onlookers thought, "There is just another white woman gone bad." I was abducted in exactly the same way as Deborah Sykes! But Willard Brown was the only one that abducted me.

It was crucial information to include in the police report. However, when I asked him to add these facts, Miller told me that those types of details would be addressed if the case ever went to court.

How discouraging! It seemed to me that Miller could

select whatever pieces of the story he wanted to include in the report. Nothing I said changed his mind.

The one other detail that he did not put in the report was the extreme violent character of my attacker. Brown was capable of violent behavior, and there were more similarities between my attack and Deborah's attack.

Eyewitnesses to the Sykes murder stated that Deborah was on her hands and knees. I was also forced to be on my hands and knees, which is another similarity between our cases that was totally ignored. Robbery seemed to be another similarity.

After I positively identified Willard Brown in the lineup, Detective Crump asked me if I wanted to press charges. He told me there was only a 50/50 chance of a conviction because it was my word against Brown's word, and there was no other conclusive evidence. He also stated that, "If convicted, Brown would be out of jail in three years, four years, five years maximum was his estimation." Brown was out when I was attacked, but said to be living in High Point. Brown was said to be in prison when Deborah was killed.

This was a tough blow for me. The investigators did not believe that all the physical evidence they collected at the crime scene, along with my identification of Brown was sufficient to convict the man of kidnapping, rape, armed robbery, and attempted murder, and that, if convicted, he would only get three to five years. Surely, my life and the brutality I had experienced were worth more punishment than that.

I told Detective Crump the time Brown served would be just enough to piss him off, so that he would come back and kill me.

For years afterward, I kept just a few papers in a yellow folder. Detective Crump had told me that sometimes you have to file everything in a box and put it away on a shelf in a closet. Sometimes you might have to take it out, look at it and sort things, and rearrange it and then eventually it goes back on the shelf.

He was drawing a word picture for me to try to cope with the situation. There was no way that I could have done anything differently that morning of February 2, 1985. I was not at fault, and could not have possibly known what was going to happen to me that day.

As I left the Police Department in 1989, I stood face to face with Detective Crump. My last recollection of my words to him were, "Wouldn't it be wild if one day we found out that the same person that got me was the same person that killed Deborah Sykes?"

That same day, Detective Crump asked me if I would like to speak with his superior, Furman Mason. I said, "Yes." I was invited into his office and sat face-to-face with him as we talked about my case. He told me how lucky I was to be alive, and I agreed.

Furman Mason and I discussed the Police Department's inactive but open cases. He assured me that these were not forgotten cases, and at that time, he pulled a list of cases off the side wall behind his desk. He assured me that these cases were still open, and that they were continuing to seek leads to solve these cases. He was comforting me and trying to reassure me that the cases, although technically inactive, were still being worked on. Furman Mason knew about my case, and he confirmed this by allowing me to see this information also.

Prior to Darryl Hunt's second trial, during a re-investigation, Detective Crump told me that I needed to get on with my life. He told me I was fortunate to be alive, and that Deborah Sykes had died. He said that I still have my life, and can go on with my husband, have kids, and a future. Deborah could not do that.

I felt that he was trying to make me feel guilty for pursuing Willard Brown because I escaped death. They discouraged me from prosecuting. The way the investigation of my case was handled, and how I was treated throughout the investigation, were the primary reasons I did not press charges against Willard Brown. There was distrust, and I was told they could not help me prove my case.

When I considered what I *thought* were true facts, it contributed greatly to my decision not to prosecute Brown. I was told that Brown was in prison when Sykes was raped and killed. The police record that was shown to me did not show a gun charge, even though it was actually the first charge on Brown's record, and I specifically asked if he had a prior gun charge. I wonder where my police report was all of these years. Was it locked up?

What about the two eyewitnesses, Mrs. Cotton and Mr. Wagner? Mrs. Cotton told investigators that she saw me driving the yellow Volkswagen, and she saw the black man in the passenger seat beside me.

The police did not go back and question Mrs. Cotton again. They did not show her the composite drawing of Willard Brown. The detectives said during Mrs. Cotton's interview that she could not identify him; however, they did not show her any other photo lineups, or do anything at all to find out if she could identify the man.

Detective Miller misled me, and told me that he personally went back and talked to Mr. Wagner. He told me that Mr. Wagner said he did not see anything. Miller never returned to talk to Mr. Wagner; therefore, Wagner was never questioned by detectives, only the police on the day of the attack. It was important to me for Detective Miller to tell Mr. Wagner "thank you."

Miller could have easily arranged for an official statement and questioning session with Wagner, and might have been able to find evidence to help me convict Willard Brown. What if he had returned with another victim in the woods!

Many times throughout the first year of the investigation, I contacted the police department, and provided them with details and requests that could help in the arrest of Willard Brown. Detective Crump said, " *Due to other job assignments, I was unable to work on your case as much as necessary.*"

In fact, this is documented in the Police Reports. In August 1985, I asked Detective Crump if he could videotape specific areas of downtown Winston-Salem where Brown was known to hangout. In the police report dated September 12, 1985, Crump stated, "Due to other job assignments, I have been unable to contact Lane for interview." He also stated that he asked Detective Johnson to videotape areas of downtown the week of 9/2 and 9/6/85.

However, this never took place. There was no follow-through at all. I did not understand why there was so little being done to catch my attacker, and why they did not seem interested in helping me pursue justice for the evils that were inflicted on me.

There are many reasons as to why I made the decision not to pursue charges against Willard Brown at the time. These are some of the major reasons.

By looking through the window at Willard Brown, I was 80%-85% sure he was my attacker. However, the primary reason I did not press charges was the Detectives and Investigators intimidated me and pressured me to back away from the case by the information that was given to me.

I do not feel that I have to justify my decision not to press charges against Brown to other people. It was the best decision for me at that time. I want to provide all the details regarding my rationale at the time so that others will understand why I chose to move on with my life.

When it came down to deciding whether to press charges against Brown, I weighed all the evidence that the police had. Basically, they had nothing except for my identification of Willard Brown. I needed to be absolutely certain that I was doing the right thing, and that there was enough evidence to gain a conviction.

According to what the police were telling me at the time, I did not believe I could prove my case. It required the detectives to bring the case forward, but it was obvious they could not give me what I needed to press forward.

They could not provide concrete evidence. Like I said before, they heard me, but they did not fully listen to me.

I was convinced that I needed to be 100% sure before I pressed charges against another human being. My nature is to give people the benefit-of-the-doubt, and I knew that I would have wanted to be treated that way if the roles were reversed.

I believe in "do unto others as you would have them do unto you." I believe in mercy, tolerance, and forgiveness.

Do I forgive Willard Brown for what he did to me? Yes, I forgive him. He was a desperate, self-gratifying man that day.

Now, I want to reach out to other victims and help them find comfort and assurance when faced with similar horrific circumstances in their lives.

People have to live with their decisions for *the rest of their lives*. I am convinced that I made the right decision for me at the time. Now, it has come full circle thanks to dedicated people, and the truth is finally being uncovered. God has a time and place for full disclosure of what happened to me. This is what I have prayed for. I left it in God's hands and prayed for His will to be done.

Now is that time.

To sum it all up, there were multiple reasons for my decision. I was led to believe that Willard Brown was in prison when Deborah Sykes was murdered, which I later found out was untrue. In addition, the police mistakenly told me that Willard Brown never had anything on his police record about gun possession. We now know that he did have a 1982 conviction for gun possession.

The police detectives' actions and statements made me feel like I was not a priority. In numerous documented police reports, detectives stated that their workload was too heavy to spend adequate time on my case. I question this because, according to published accounts of the Deborah Sykes investigation, there were at least 260 police officers, detectives, and investigators working to solve her murder. If there were 260 resources available at that time, it seems to me that more people could have been assigned to my case.

One of the downfalls in my investigation was switching detectives after three months. There have never been any addendums to my case reports to correct what was documented incorrectly.

One of the most important steps would be for detectives or another police employee to review a case with the victim. This would bring clarity, correctness, and possibly new comparisons.

I asked Detective Miller if there were other rapes similar

to mine in the same timeframe, and he told me he did not know of any but that other detectives might be working on cases. The fact is that Miller was also involved in the Sykes case, and had knowledge of the similarities between the Linda E case of June 13-14, 1984, Kathleen's case on January 1, 1985, in addition to my case of February, 1985 and Deborah's case.

There were so many similarities between the Sykes case and mine. When I asked about this, I was told that they did not want to do anything to jeopardize their case against Darryl Hunt for the murder of Deborah Sykes, and did not want to ask questions that would put doubt in people's minds about Hunt's guilt. According to discovery evidence and opinions of the Review Committee, the composite drawing of my attacker was almost identical to the composite drawing from the Sykes murder eyewitness descriptions. These two drawings should logically have been compared. Looking back, we now know that is exactly what needed to happen!

The police did not draw a comparison between the atrocities done to Deborah and to me. The manner of abduction was identical; the police never documented the manner in which I was abducted. In addition, they did not conduct a detailed search for evidence from the scene of my abduction.

There were misleading and wrong statements documented in the police record about my case. The official report states that I was raped outside the car, which is not true. Detective Miller's report contained inconsistent statements. One example is he states I "did as ordered" and removed Brown's belt. This was not true.

At the start of the investigation of my case, we asked the police to use K9's to track my attacker. They said it would be too difficult because of the rain; however, that was not true. In fact, per the experts, using a K9 to track the scent is easier and more effective in these types of weather conditions.

I also asked the police to conduct a Voice Recognition test, but they refused, explaining it was too expensive.

Voice Recognition is as good as a fingerprint when used as evidence in a court of law. Detective Crump knew and I knew that Willard Brown had a deep, gruff voice. We agreed on that!

Police never documented the violent character of my attacker, even though I discussed it multiple times. Detective Crump told me that violence was not in Brown's nature. Early on, I asked Detective Miller to pursue an attempted murder charge in addition to kidnapping, armed robbery, and rape. He said, "We'll see," but the charge was not added. Twenty-one years and one day later, I finally received my police report.

All the physical evidence in my case was destroyed, including the rape kit, glove, blood samples, the bus transfer and ticket, footprint casts, and lab results. All these things could be DNA tested today if they were available. Actually, even though they had the footprint casts and were able to identify the type of shoes Brown was wearing, they did not do a comparison on the shoe size prints to Brown's foot.

Detective Miller told me that he talked to Mr. Wagner after my attack, and that Wagner said he did not see anything. Actually, I did not know until years later that Detective Miller never went back to see Mr. Wagner. The detectives also did not show the composite drawing to any of the eyewitnesses to my case, including Mrs. Cotton who saw me and Brown in my yellow Volkswagen driving into the woods. Why didn't detectives return to the area with the composite of my attacker?

I asked if the composite pictures were taken back to the apartment complex. The drawing was not shown to any of the residents of the apartment complex.

When I contemplated pressing charges against Brown, I was told that the police could not help me prove my case. They discouraged me from pressing charges, stating there was only a 50/50 chance of a conviction, and that it was my word against Brown's word.

I was told Brown, his girlfriend Freida (last name unknown), and another couple, the Thomas family, lived in High Point during this time, which Brown's mother confirmed. This piece of information was somehow supposed to convince me that Brown could not have committed the crime.

Prior to Darryl's second trial in 1989, Detective Crump even told me to get on with my life. They made me feel guilty to be alive when Deborah was dead.

I felt ignored, neglected, and that my attack was insignificant in light of the more politically charged Sykes murder case. Eric Saunders, the Assistant District Attorney, told me that I needed professional help to gain closure.

Those are the primary reasons I decided not to pursue charges against Willard Brown. I was 19-years-old, and at times, felt like I was all alone in trying to solve my case. I did not feel that I had adequate police support and protection, and that sufficient investigation had been conducted to help me prove my case against Brown.

Even pondering the arrest, I waited ten months for the man I picked out of a picture lineup to be arrested. They did not arrest Brown for my crime. They brought him in for questioning on the Deborah Sykes case. Years later, I found out that my case was never included in Deborah's case. Early on, Willard Brown denied killing Deborah too!

I can only wonder who was actually in charge of the investigations, and planning the next move as 1984 was a political year.

Regina K. Lane and Dr. Linda F. Felker

CHAPTER FOUR

27 Years as the Integon Victim

Proverbs 3:5-6
Trust in the LORD with all your heart, with all your body, and with all your soul. Lean not unto your own understanding, and he will direct your path.

The Winston-Salem Journal and Sentinel first reported my attack on Monday, February 5, 1985. They labeled me "The Integon Victim" because they were not allowed to release my name to the public.

That name was used to describe me for 27 years. I did not grant an official interview to the newspapers or other media during those years because I did not press charges against Willard Brown. My identity was protected. (Once I agreed to an interview and the Sykes Commission Report was complete, I believed it was time to tell the whole story. I wanted to make sure that everyone understands the reasons for my decision.)

I knew it weighed heavily on professional people's minds that I did not prosecute Willard Brown, and that there were probably people who blamed me because they did not understand all the circumstances.

The way the Winston-Salem Journal & Sentinel reported the activities of my case, and my decision, was not fair. It seemed like a pressure tactic to force me to reveal my identity, in addition to pressing charges against Brown.

It should not take a newspaper to force a police department to do its job. The Winston-Salem Journal &

Sentinel assigned their own reporters to the Sykes case to try to find the killer. They did not assign a special investigative reporter to my case to find my attacker.

It was not that I did not want to prosecute; I wanted to make sure that I was 100% right. I felt like I was holding another person's life in my hands, and I decided to analyze the situation in reverse. What if it was me? How would I want to be treated? Would I want someone to prosecute me if the police had no concrete evidence?

Think again of the answers I received to all the questions I asked the police detectives. Their answers were vague, non-committal and, in many instances, very false answers. Still, I trusted them without reserve, and I let the police handle the investigation the way they chose to proceed. I was made to believe they were working in my best interest in an honest and professional manner.

I believed then, as I believe now, that God has a timetable for my life. It was not the right time to disclose many of the facts I am telling now. At this point in my life, the circumstances have changed dramatically, and, at last, the door is wide open for me to explain what happened.

Three years prior, I had started the disclosure process by telling my experience to my two best friends at work, Julie Kerley and Penny Clinard. I also shared with my current boss, Chris Stanfield, and my manager, Becky Moore, who was my best friend in 1985, and still is today. They, along with Maggie Haney, Linda Felker, and many others, gave me a safe and supportive environment to talk about the attack and subsequent events. They are dear friends and very special ladies.

I also told the Faith Harmony Quartet, made up of two retired firefighters from the City of Winston-Salem, Sam Spencer and Leo Gower, and my best friend, Lisa Davis. I love to stand next to her and sing. Our quartet has sung together since 1999.

I assisted the Sykes Administrative Review Committee to uncover the truth of how my case and the Sykes case were investigated, beginning in 1984, and continuing until today.

Many people look at what happened to me, and express

horror and disbelief that I actually survived the attack. More than that, they wonder how I was able to move on with my life, and if I have endured years of intolerable mental anguish because of February 2, 1985. Like the movie Groundhog Day, I relived this day repeatedly.

Certainly, it was a traumatic experience, and one that I will never forget. My mind just could not comprehend that a person could be so mean to another human being. There has never been a doubt in my mind that Willard Brown intended to kill me, and if I had not tucked my chin down at just the right moment, he would have sliced my throat wide open. Willard Brown had no self-control.

God was in control throughout the entire fight. It was not in God's plan for me to die that day. This is such a comforting thought to know that regardless of what that evil man planned to do, God had his seal of protection on my life. I only wish Deborah could have lived too!

Many people have asked why I lived and Deborah died. I answer, "I don't know." Deborah was beautiful on the outside and beautiful on the inside. The Bible tells us that God knows and looks at our hearts.

Deborah was described by her mother, Mrs. Evelyn Jefferson, as a wonderful Christian woman, who loved the Lord Jesus. She enjoyed sewing, singing in the choir, and volunteer work. She gave so much in her life, and yet her life was cut so short with her family and her husband, Doug.

My life verse is Proverbs 3:5-6: *Trust in the Lord with all your heart, with all your body, and with all your soul. Lean not unto your own understanding, and he will direct your path."*

This scripture reference is the kitchen border in my house, and was there when we bought the house. This verse has brought comfort and assurance to my soul. I **know** without a doubt that God is in control of my life. He has been gracious to allow me to mature twenty years in my walk with Him.

I want to proclaim to you that **God is Good**. My life, though not perfect, has been filled with tremendous blessings. Yes, there have been trials, but I have sometimes fasted during those trials and prayed, allowing God's will to be done in my life.

As I look back on the last 22 years, I am amazed at how God has brought me forward to this point. I am amazed at how His hand has directed each step that I have taken, and I am amazed at His provision.

God has been with me every moment. He has guided and orchestrated each situation of my life, and provided multiple opportunities for me to grow spiritually, emotionally, and mentally.

I believe that He *allowed* situations in my life in order to prepare me for what He is getting ready to do through me. I say *allowed* rather than *ordered* because God is so merciful to his children. He would not dictate and instruct Willard Brown to attack me. However, He would allow it to happen to for a variety of reasons.

God can use my situation to encourage my faith. He proved His love, power, and strength by giving me the characteristics I needed to survive. God was faithful to me. He never left me, and I could feel His love and presence throughout the ordeal.

God used this situation to teach me to live in His word and depend on His guidance. As I look back at specific developments in my personal and professional life, I can see the hand of God moving.

God used my suffering to prepare me to help other suffering people. I know what it feels like to be abducted; I know what it feels like to be brutalized; I know what it feels like to be victimized.

When God allows these circumstances in your life, there will always be a future opportunity to use the experience to share His marvelous protective power and grace to help someone who may be in the same situation.

There are so many hurting people in this world, whether victims of crime, or victims of their own actions. No matter what the circumstance or what you are going through, people need the Lord!

God has prepared me to help others through my

testimony. He has given me a tender heart, compassion, and understanding. And, I want to use what He has taught me to reach others for Jesus Christ.

Throughout the last 27 years, my life has been full, but not easy. When God is at work in the hearts and lives of His children, it does not mean that there will never be heartache, or trouble. It means that He will provide comfort, support, and resolution to those who seek His will. Just like the words in Ginny Owens' song, "If You Want Me To." He never said it would be easy; He only said I would never go alone.

If You Want Me To
The pathway is broken
And the signs are unclear
And I don't know the reason
Why You brought me here.
But just because You love me the way that You do
I'm gonna walk through the valley
If You want me to.

'Cause I'm not who I was
When I took my first step
And I'm clinging to the promise
You're not through with me yet.
So, if all of these trials bring me closer to you
Then I will walk through the fire
If You want me to.

It may not be the way I would have chosen
When you lead me through a world that's not my home.
But You never said it would be easy
You only said I'd never go alone.

So when the whole world turns against me
And I'm all by myself,
And I can't hear You answer my cries for help.
I'll remember the suffering
Your love put You through,
And I will go through the valley
If You want me to

The day after Willard Brown's trial in December 2004, I received the kindest email from the President and CEO of the company I work for today. The email was supportive, encouraging, and loving. God placed me in this workplace because He knew I would need the acceptance, understanding, and support of a dedicated employer and boss. I had the support of many of my Triad Guaranty colleagues, especially the people in Customer Service. Many of the people in the company are people I worked with twenty years ago.

Each step of my life, every change in my circumstances, has been orchestrated and controlled by God. My trust and faith rest fully in Him, and He has been so faithful to me. I long to serve Him, and have purposed in my heart to maintain a willing and obedient attitude toward the things of the Lord. Yes, I do fear the Lord.

Two weeks after Willard Brown attacked me, I went back to work at Integon. I was scared and wondered if I would be safe. The Security Officers at Integon instituted safety measures, which gave me a reasonable amount of reassurance that it was all right to go back to work.

My life did not stop after returning to my position at Integon. One very special memory is of the Bridal Shower that the employees of Integon Insurance had for me during my engagement. There was food and presents, and so many good wishes from some truly special friends. I know that a great deal of time and energy went into planning our celebration, and they reached out to share their love and blessings. They provided so many of the things that we needed to start our new life together.

Scott and I were married in May 1985. God blessed our family, and I was determined to put the past behind us and move forward to provide a loving, nurturing home for our children.

I remember many years ago, I stood in the kitchen and prayed for God to allow us to buy a home. We were pre-approved at the bank, and looking for a home we could afford that would meet the needs of our family.

My husband actually found our home in a really

unconventional way. He stopped by a yard sale one morning, and had to drive down the road to turn around. The current owner, Richard Howell, a Pastoral Counselor, was placing a "for sale" sign in the front yard, and Scott stopped to inquire. Shortly thereafter, we moved into our house. What a wonderful blessing from the Lord! Prayer does change things.

I continued to work at Integon Insurance Company for several years, and then accepted a position with the Investment Life Insurance Company of America as a Unit Leader. This promotional opportunity allowed me to develop my skills and work with people to enhance their own capabilities. Again, I believe God provided this unique challenge in my life to prepare me for His service. I specifically believe that now, 27 years after the attack, I can use these skills to help other victims, and counsel people to serve Him.

After three years with Investment Life, I returned to Integon Life Insurance. They were happy to welcome me back to the company, and I continued working there until Integon Life was sold in 1995. One hour later, I walked into my next job.

God opened the door for me to work at Rosemont Baptist Church School. What a glorious time those years were! I was the school secretary, church secretary, office manager, cook, cleaner, pre-school director, and acting Christian Principal for many years. I enjoyed serving and helping people.

It is amazing to look back at that time in my life and realize God's hand in my career choices. He developed my skills at the insurance companies and taught me how to communicate effectively with people. At the church, He taught me process and administrative skills, payroll, and accounting.

What a combination! It is clear to me now that He gave me opportunities to learn through experience the qualities that I need today. As I move forward with accepting the next stages of my life, I am convinced that God will use the interpersonal skills, communication abilities, and leadership qualities that He developed in me to further the cause of Christ. Moreover, I know that I will be able to use my expertise in ways that will help other people. That is my heart's desire.

God has brought me to this place in my life, and it is the right time to open up and reveal the details of what happened to me. As you will read in the following chapters, I have been very willing to discuss my experience with the Sykes Administrative Review committee in hopes of finding the truth and more pieces of life's puzzle.

In addition, God has given me an opportunity to tell the world about His marvelous love and amazing grace. I was asked by Ricki Stern and Annie Sundburg of Break Thru Films to participate in a documentary film entitled "The Trials of Darryl Hunt." I agreed to provide five hours of interview time, and allow the crew to film me singing at church, both solo and with our great choir! The proceeds of this documentary were donated to a non-profit organization established in Darryl Hunt's name, to help victims who are wrongly convicted of crime.

I felt it imperative to share my experience with my church family and discussed it with my pastor, Ed Sears and Minister of Music, Mark Walker. I was allowed to speak to the choir one evening during rehearsal.

On Wednesday evening, **July 12, 2006**, I stood before the Grace Baptist Temple choir, and told them a portion of my story. I asked them to support me as I began what would, hopefully be the conclusion of this part of my story, and the beginning of another incredible journey to bring knowledge of the Lord Jesus Christ to a needy world.

This is what I said to the choir that night.

To The Grace Baptist Temple Choir:

I will first ask how many people have lived in Winston-Salem or the surrounding areas for the last 20-25 years?

I come to you today as my Brothers and Sisters in the Lord Jesus Christ, asking that you DO NOT disclose what I am about to tell you, but to walk with me on this incredible journey God has me on.

Growing up on a farm in Michigan life was quiet and peaceful. It was uneventful until the day I remember running to my mother after my oldest brother climbed a tree to free a cat, while my older brother threw a rock upward trying to scare the cat down.

I remember this first trauma in my life. At that age, just old enough to open a door, I ran into the house saying, "MOM, MOM, Fred's forehead just fell off. Well, it did not fall off but he was definitely hurt and needed help. There were also no three-second rules for lollipops back then either, as my dad so often reminds me on a video he took.

Sometimes I wonder how I survived being kicked in the mouth by a wild pony, knocking all of my teeth loose. In addition, I was riding double with my Aunt Cindy on our favorite pony Sunshine and the pony fell breaking my right arm. I had on my favorite little sailor's bathing suit that day and begged the doctor at the hospital not to cut it off but he had to in order to re-break my arm and reset it.

Little did I know that my left arm would one-day help save my life.

Before we moved from Charlotte, Michigan, we attended the First Baptist Church of Charlotte. Our favorite songs our family sang growing up were "Jesus Loves Me" and "You Are My Sunshine." This is where at the age of 5-6 I accepted Jesus as my personal Savior in junior church. I went forward knowing that salvation was a free gift. My older brother Tom accepted Christ the Sunday before as I watched.

I learned that Jesus would forgive me for the bad things I thought and I could live with Him in a wonderful place called Heaven. On September 6, 1970, I watched as my father, oldest brother Fred, older brother Tom were all baptized. My mother also joined the church based on experience. I am happy to say that today, our whole family has accepted the Lord Jesus Christ as their Savior.

Shortly thereafter, my father transferred to New Jersey with Owens-Illinois, which provided us with the things we required in life. We were moving back to family and friends.

We lived there until 1975, my 9th birthday. Owens then transferred my father to Winston-Salem, NC, where my family continues to live today. This is also where our family had our sweet little Tarheel bonus, Rebecca Pearl.

Life seemed normal, growing up playing basketball, volleyball, softball. Softball was definitely my favorite sport. From the age of 13-16, I played on a team with my younger sister Trish. She was an awesome shortstop. I had the wonderful job of pitching left handed. At 16, about to age out of the league, our team was again undefeated and we went to the State Championships.

Oh what fun memories, great experiences learning teamwork and a good way to build the strength in my arms. Life changes at 16 when you get your license, start driving, and land a first job.

In 1982, I graduated from North Davidson High School in Welcome, NC, and started working at a big insurance company in downtown Winston-Salem. Wanting to be independent, even though I had the best of everything at home, I moved in with a girlfriend, and we rented a one-bedroom apartment. I wanted to know I could take care of myself before I cared for a family.

Life was good, working full time, and meeting a man I fell in love with and had become engaged to. I received another promotion at work, which required weekend work.

On a Saturday morning in February, 21 years ago, I parked my car about 8:00 a.m. in the Integon parking lot, and walked toward the building. A man reached the steps at the same time as I did, and I spoke to him, saying hello, just as I would to any other person.

He grabbed me, and as much as I struggled, I never made it to work that day. Instead, I was dragged away at gunpoint, badly beaten, robbed, and worse, much worse. I will not go into the details of that horrible day, but I will tell you that what happened to me is part of one of the most highly publicized cases in Winston-Salem today.

In December 2003, I learned from a Winston-Salem Detective and an SBI agent that the person I picked from a police lineup in 1986, Willard Brown, was the same person that had also raped and killed newspaper editor, Deborah Sykes.

In December 2004, I was present in the courtroom with my mother and the Sykes family when the judge sentenced Willard Brown for the murder of Deborah Sykes. Since then, I have been asked many times to be interviewed for articles in the Winston-Salem Journal, which I always declined.

I have met and interviewed with police personnel, Mark Rabil, the defense attorney for Darryl Hunt and his investigator, Richard McGough.

Most recently after sharing my story with the Sykes Administrative Review Committee, I was asked to interview and film part of a documentary with Ricki Stern, who is a female, and works with Break Thru Films in New York. Ricki worked for HBO for six years. Everyone that has heard my story knows that the Lord Jesus Christ was my divine intervention during the attack, and only by the grace of God am I here today to attest to His love, my life, and my faith in Jesus.

I have committed five hours to Ricki for an interview and filming next week, July 19th. Ricki knows that I love to sing and she loves choir music. I ask you now if you will meet me here next Wednesday for us to give our statement of faith to the world? The film will travel to Spain, Ireland, France, Belgium, the European Film Festival and more.

I am working to bring closure to my situation. Dr. Linda Felker has agreed to work on a book of my story, as we discussed at her home two nights ago. Thank you Maggie Haney for praying and being with Linda Felker and me that night as we started plans for this book.

After suppressing this information for so many years, opening up seems to be the best way to complete my healing process. I have a close relationship with Deborah Syke's mother, Evelyn Jefferson and I just do not want to carry the burden alone anymore. I hope to help in the healing of hurting people. I am hoping to help victims and the families of victims.

Those are some of the things we plan to address in the book. I also hope that the Sykes Administrative Review

Committee may be able to help us all to know what went wrong.

Many of you wondered why I became so emotional on February 1st of this year after our choir sang the beautiful song "By The Way of The Cross", and The Prestonwood choir song "I Will Sing Praise." My heart was so full. I left the choir crying, knowing that the next day I would face the police, the press, the committee, and many more people that are important in order to share my experience.

Please pray for this situation and work with me to find a positive way to tell the world about our Savior. I can stand by in silence letting people around me say what they think they need to say, or I can open up, share my experience, and hope that God will use it for praise and to glorify His name.

I am glad that Ricki Stern, Mark Rabil, and Richard McGough felt my story was a powerful, untold story.

CHAPTER FIVE

The Big Picture

<u>Exodus 15:2</u>
The Lord is my strength. He has become my salvation. He is my God, and I will praise Him. I will exalt Him.

<u>Romans 8:28</u>
And we know that all things work together for good to them that love God, to them who are the called according to his purpose.

There has been a tremendous amount of media coverage on the Deborah Sykes rape and murder. Throughout the investigation of her case, hundreds of police officers, investigators, SBI, detectives, and investigative reporters, politicians, and citizens were involved in solving the crime.

My attack happened six months after Deborah died. I knew there had to be a connection between my case and Deborah Sykes' case; the evidence absolutely pointed to this conclusion. However, every time I asked the detectives about the possibility that Darryl Hunt was innocent, and that my attacker actually committed both crimes, I was told that they were sure there was no connection. I was told the main reason for their assumption was my attacker's height, and that the Sykes' killer was taller.

I explained that my attacker appeared to be 5'6"to 5'9" tall, but could be taller because he had grabbed me around the neck and pulled me down. This could alter my perception of his height. In addition, I was wearing shoes with 1" heels that morning, which could also explain the variance in height perception.

I identified Willard Brown as my attacker, both in a photographic lineup and a live lineup. Again, I asked if any comparisons had been made to determine if Brown could have also attacked Deborah. Again, the answer was no, because Brown was in jail. We now know that this was false information.

However, there was a bigger part of the story that I did not know about, and that the newspapers and other media did not know.

There were actually four attacks in eight months, all in approximately the same vicinity during the period of June 14, 1984, and February 2, 1985.

1. 6/13-14/1984: A white female was abducted at gunpoint from 500 West Fifth Street, and raped several times. (This is the location of the Integon Building, now GMAC, and the same place where I was abducted). Her attacker was a black male approximately 25 years old, and around 5' 3" tall.She managed to escaped and notified police at 3:31 a.m.

2. 8/10/1984: Deborah Sykes was abducted, raped, stabbed, and murdered in downtown Winston-Salem, near Crystal Towers (about 2 blocks from Fifth Street). Darryl Hunt was found guilty of this crime, and spent 18 years in prison convicted of rape and first-degree murder.

3. 1/1/1985: A white female reported she was raped on N. Hawthorne Road by a black male. Her case was closed on 1/31/85 (one month later!) due to lack of investigative leads. All evidence in the case was destroyed.

4. 2/2/85: I was kidnapped at gunpoint from the side of the Integon Building, also at 500 West Fifth Street in downtown Winston-Salem. I was raped, stabbed 12 times, robbed, and almost killed. I identified Willard Brown in a photographic lineup in May 1985 and in a live line-up in March 1986. My case was closed due to lack of investigative evidence, and all physical evidence in the case

was destroyed.

If we look at the specific details in each one of these cases, a pattern emerges that is impossible to overlook. The first rape took place beginning the evening of June 13, 1984, and continuing until the early hours of June 14, 1985. The victim immediately reported the assault, and provided the investigating officers with a description of her attacker. She was dubbed "Linda E." by investigators through the police reports, and her identity was not revealed.

Linda E. reported that she was abducted at gunpoint by a black male, approximately 25 years old. She was raped several times, in several places in the downtown Winston-Salem area, including the park behind Crystal Towers across West End Boulevard. This is the approximate vicinity of the Deborah Sykes murder, and a couple of blocks from where I was kidnapped.

Her case was assigned to Detective Teresa Hicks, an expert in handling rape cases. Hicks documented the file that she tried to call Linda E. on June 15, and then left for 12 days of vacation. Hicks wrote that she "was unable to *attempt* to contact the victim" because she was on vacation.

The question is simple: were there no other detectives available who could begin an immediate investigation into this crime? Linda E. provided the police with a report of the attack, and submitted to a rape examination by medical professionals. She provided police with a detailed description of the events, beginning in the evening of June 13, and continuing until she escaped in the early morning hours of June 14.

However, Detective Hicks went away on vacation and did nothing to investigate the crime scene, or gather any evidence, until at least two weeks later.

Shortly thereafter, Linda E. moved out of town, disheartened and discouraged by the lack of police support. The police destroyed Linda E.'s rape kit evidence on September 5, 1984, and destroyed all the clothing evidence on September 8, 1984.

This evidence was destroyed while Linda E.'s case was

still open! Naturally, this was against all prevailing police policy at that time. Evidence is never destroyed while the case is still active and the investigation is continuing! The evidence was destroyed one week before Darryl Hunt was arrested and charged with the murder of Deborah Sykes on September 14, 1984.

Today, Linda says she felt guilty for years over her situation. Police were stating that she left town and then they closed her investigation. But, in reality, her case was closed before she left town.

Destroying the evidence made it more difficult to proceed with solving the Linda E. case. But, it also made finding any connection between the two cases more difficult.

One obvious similarity between Linda E.'s case and my case is that the police insinuated that they did not believe her story. Linda E. was given a polygraph test, which she passed, to prove she was telling the truth. The police did not take her claim of rape seriously, even though she reported it immediately.

Similarly, as I stated before, Detective Miller made comments to me that indicated he might not believe that I was abducted and raped. He said to me that he "had to be sure I wasn't making it up." I was very offended when he said that, and began to wonder if the police department was going to take my case seriously and ever find the man that attacked me.

Another curious reporting similarity between the Linda E. case and my case is the way the police reports were documented regarding our whereabouts. Linda E.'s report states that she moved away, and the detective was unable to contact her. My own police reports also documented when I changed addresses right after I was married in May 1985, and again later in the investigation.

In both our police reports, those comments appear to be written in an effort to discredit us as witnesses. There was a lack of communication between Detectives Miller and Crump when there was a change in lead detectives. In my report, the statement that I moved was not completed with comments about 'why' I moved, and would lead the reader to believe that I was not a reliable witness. I still worked at the same place, and they could have easily contacted me there, as they did so many times.

Linda E. told detectives that her attacker was approximately 5'3" – 5'4", which is close to the same information I provided to them about my attacker. He kidnapped both of us at gunpoint, and threatened to kill both of us.

Linda E.'s attacker told her that he just got out of prison. Her attack happened on June 13 and 14, which is around the time that Willard Brown was released from jail.

Of course, I was told that Willard Brown was still in jail, and that Brown could not be connected to the Sykes case. But, considering what we now know about the actual release date of Willard Brown, it is entirely possible that Brown could have been involved in the Linda E. case, as well as my case. It is a logical conclusion considering that he later admitted to raping and murdering Deborah Sykes, but only a DNA match proved that he was guilty.

Detective Teresa Hicks was working Linda E.'s case when Deborah Sykes was murdered, and was at the scene of the crime with other investigators after the murder of Deborah Sykes.

I wonder if the detectives solely considered the height of the attackers in each case, and said that is why they believed they were different attackers.

The SBI report of 1986 documents that various police personnel commented to Hicks that there might be possible similarities between the two cases. In addition, Detective Bill Miller, who was the primary first detective assigned to investigate my case from February 2, 1985, until May 1985, was also involved in investigating the Linda E. and Sykes cases.

Why was there no immediate comparison of the evidence between the three cases? There is documented evidence that these people knew of all the rape cases. However, when I specifically asked Detective Miller if there were other cases similar to mine under investigation, he said "No, but there might be other detectives working on other cases."

The media was never informed of the Linda E. rape. According to testimony from previous reporters with the Winston-Salem Journal and Winston-Salem Sentinel, they did not know about the Linda D. or the Kathleen D. rapes. If they had been aware of those crimes, it surely would have been reported in the newspaper.

It was not until December 2003 that the media found out about the Linda E. story, and the possible connection to the Sykes investigation. It took Linda E. calling the news station, and the news station calling the Police Department. Then, someone said, "You better talk to this lady."

The triangle of 'connect the dots' between these cases is obvious. The third victim in January of 1985 was dubbed, "Kathleen D." She also abducted, raped, and threatened in the downtown vicinity, at Brunson Elementary. She died in 2005, and a suspect was never arrested in her case. However, it must be mentioned that there are obvious similarities present in her case as well.

To begin with, there was no press coverage. No one even knew about that rape. This is so odd, given the commonalities inherent in these cases. However, when I remember how adamant the detectives were about the lack of connection between my case and the Sykes, it is a natural assumption that there would have been no attempt to connect the January 1985 rape with any of the other three rapes.

There were four potentially related attacks. The first was Linda E. in June 1984, then Deborah Sykes in August 1984. Kathleen D. was next in January 1985, and my attack was February 1985.

To add clarity between these four cases, it must be noted that only the Deborah Sykes has been solved, and that Willard Brown confessed to raping and murdering her. He has refused to be interviewed about the other three rape cases, and denied attacking me.

The other three cases were all closed; not one suspect was ever arrested in connection with these brutal attacks. My mind is boggled with the inconsistencies inherent in these four cases.

So much attention was given to prosecuting and convicting Darryl Hunt for the murder of Deborah Sykes. Why was so little done to arrest and prosecute the man who attacked the other three women? Why were no investigative leads found?

Again, I refer to the questions I asked Detectives Miller and Crump specifically about Willard Brown, and could he be the same one that murdered Deborah Sykes. Each time I asked the question, I was told that eyewitnesses said Deborah's attackers were tall men.

Many times, I explained how the height of the attacker could be different, based on your actual viewpoint in relation to where you are standing. As I said before, I was being held around the neck, and pulled down. But, they would not consider my explanation, and insisted Deborah's attackers were too tall to be the same one who assaulted me.

We now know that Darryl Hunt was not the right man; Willard Brown was the man who killed Sykes. He admitted that he did it, and he did it alone. Brown was also the man who kidnapped, raped, beat, robbed and tried to kill me.

Maybe alcohol, drugs, and other substances kept Willard Brown's from remembering my attack. However, this is certainly no excuse for what he did to me.

For years, the newspaper has written articles and stories about "The Integon Victim", and I can only wonder if people thought that I was partly to blame for Hunt's incarceration for 18 years because I refused to come forward. As recently as August 6, 2006, there was an article in the Winston-Salem Journal that included comments inferring that, had I prosecuted Brown, the detectives would have been forced to review the Hunt conviction. If Brown was questioned for Deborah's crime and not mine, then why wasn't it already compared? It should have been compared in March 1986.

This is a very slanted viewpoint, and the published reports are not only unkind, they are far from the truth. From the beginning, I pressured police detectives to compare the details of my case with the details of the Sykes case. I pointed out the obvious similarities, and repeatedly asked the right questions to try to convince the police to look deeper into both of our cases.

I was ignored, patronized, and forgotten. The primary responsibility for solving my case was the detectives and investigators; however, they were more concerned with keeping Darryl Hunt in jail than finding out the truth.

It was a political year, and great pressure was being brought on the police force. Look at the letters between Chief Masten and Don Tisdale, which draw conclusions to this very fact. The policies and procedures in place at that time have since been changed to bring about a more positive and substantial method of interrogation and investigating.

Today's procedures require video and audiotaped recordings. This is a good change. It is important to understand the mentality that existed in the police department in the 80's. There was a cloak of mystery around police investigations, and newspaper journalists would not question or challenge the authority or validity of information coming from the police departments. The press creates pressure for the police department.

If the police said it, it was considered reliable information and, therefore, it was printed. Most people felt that way. The culture of the Journal and the Sentinal was not one of dissent, but of cooperation. Thank you to Phoebe Zerwick and Dan Galendo for respecting my privacy and the way I have chosen to stand quietly while the police and the Committee do their jobs.

It was extremely difficult to get information from the police, it would seem that these two organizations should work together in order to find positive and truthful results.

However, in Winston-Salem, the police keep reporters at bay. They did not provide complete reports, but only a summary sheet with limited details on any crimes committed in the city. The police and politicians did not like to advertise that there was any crime, and especially did not want to frighten citizens by announcing the possibility of a serial rapist in the community.

It seems like it was up to the reporters to remember crimes that happened, and ask the police if they were related. The police would decide if they should release information, and if so, how much. If police saw a pattern of unsolved crimes against women, they might not feel any urgency to get the warning out because of their opinions that particularly seemed to devalue women in general.

The police built a wall around their investigations, and had the notion that, only with complete secrecy will we solve crimes, which, of course, is absurd.

It appears that once law enforcement makes a mistake, they will do everything in their power to cover it up. They might withhold evidence that could exonerate a suspect, or provide half-truths to pacify victims and their families.

Therefore, for me, and Linda E., and Kathleen D., there has been no justice. We have been made to feel less important, and certainly less of a priority than the Sykes investigation. I am not saying Deborah's case was unimportant, and I pray the Sykes family will not take offense at my feelings. But, this is the way I feel. They have been through so much heartache and pain.

Throughout the years of investigations, trial, and retrial of Darryl Hunt, and the ongoing publicity naming "The Integon Victim" as being uncooperative, one fact remains true. If the detectives had listened to me, and taken action on the details that I provided, they would have certainly seen the obvious connections between these four cases.

I am not convinced that they truly did not make the connection. In my mind, I have doubt that they were sincerely trying to help me solve my case, and I doubt that they were oblivious to the connection between my case and the Sykes case. If they worked independently of each other, there might not have been comparisons.

During the last investigation with Detective Crump and the SBI in 1989, I was told that all victims were being brought back in for questioning. One statement made by Detective Crump was that "even the West End rapist victims were being re-interviewed" (white male attack on white females). I told Detective Crump this did not make sense to me.

They had to know that there was a strong possibility that there was a serial rapist in Winston-Salem, but chose to ignore it for political and professional reasons. I still wonder who was calling the shots.

It should not have to depend on me nearly being killed on February 2, 1985, and graciously offering to have my name smeared in the newspaper the next day. I have always respected the authority and trusted that they would do the right things for everyone. It is another thing if they just made a mistake. If so, confess it. Clear the air.

This experience taught me that I was wrong. I learned the hard way that I could not always trust people on this earth to protect me, or provide me with sufficient truthful answers to my questions. I could not trust them with my life, and with arresting the man who so brutally attacked me. I have suffered, but I am not the only person who has suffered.

The family of Deborah Sykes has suffered tremendously at the loss of Deborah Sykes, and at learning that the wrong man was in prison for her murder. Linda E. and Kathleen D. also suffered tremendously due to lack of attention, care, and action by the very ones who were hired to provide protection.

As for me, I continue to state the facts, and listen to the Sykes Review Committee to find out the truth of what happened, and what went wrong in the investigations.

It would be impossible to try to investigate the Sykes case, and the conviction of Willard Brown, without making the connection to my case especially since I identified Willard Brown twice! However, I was not able to press charges against him, primarily due to lack of support and discouragement from the detectives to pursue the case, and incorrect information being given to me at the time. They led me to believe they did all they could for me.

I was told that Brown was in jail when Sykes was murdered. They said they did not know that Brown had a 1982 felony charge for gun possession, even though it is the first charge on his police record. The report was never shown to me in its entirety.

The detectives told me that, if convicted for his attack of me, Brown would only receive a three-five year sentence for rape, robbery, and kidnapping. The attempted murder charge, which I asked them to add to the record, was never noted.

I did not receive a copy of my police report until 21 years later, and did not realize there was such an abundance of false information, inconsistencies, and omissions in the report. Corrections promised years earlier were not done.

I want and need closure. However, closure will not happen until everyone involved can put the pieces together and acknowledge the mistakes made, like a puzzle.

There were errors and omissions in all four cases. Now, all these years later, it is imperative that we understand the truth. We need to look at the connections between all four cases, and see the suffering and trauma that these four women and their families experienced.

The 1986 SBI report was inadequate. It was not compiled by an independent agency, but rather was written in cooperation with the Winston-Salem Police Department, inherent with their own internal investigation. How many attacks were noted?

A better investigation by the SBI in 1986 might have resulted in the Sykes case being solved correctly, and might have also led to solutions for Linda E., Kathleen D., and myself.

One of the misconceptions of the entire Big Picture and the four cases is that police investigators and detectives did not share information on the particular cases that they were working on or assigned to. Therefore, they would have had no reason to question any possible connection between the four cases.

This is grossly untrue. The Winston-Salem Police Department obviously had multiple opportunities to see the associations between these four attacks. Not only did the supervisors read and sign-off on all documentation on all cases, some of the same detectives worked on the same cases at the same time!

Teresa Hicks was involved in all of the cases, and Bill Miller worked on three of the cases, including the Sykes case and my case. They absolutely knew the details, and therefore, knew the possible connections between the cases.

There were also investigative exchange meetings every morning. At these meetings, the detectives shared with each other the details of the particular cases they were working on. These meetings were a means of communicating with each other, and an excellent method of relaying information that could have an impact on other cases under review.

As I mentioned before, all the evidence of my case was destroyed, as was the evidence in the Linda E. and Kathleen D. cases. The DNA testing methods used today could be used to analyze my rape kit, blood samples, skin cells from the glove, and other pieces of physical evidence, in order to provide positive proof of Willard Brown's guilt.

These DNA testing methods were available in 1990 and could have been used to exonerate Darryl Hunt years earlier. Willard Brown's name was excluded from any consideration because of the lack of connection between my case and the Sykes case.

The big picture tells us that there were severe mistakes made that denied justice to Darryl Hunt. The big picture also tells us that for Linda E., Kathleen D., and me, we will never have justice.

In this lifetime, I will not have complete justice for the atrocities that were perpetrated against me. But, I am not discouraged or downhearted. Christ has taught me to forgive.

My heart and mind are convinced of the authority of my Lord Jesus Christ. He is the final judge in all things. He knows the answers that we are trying to discover. If it is in His will that we uncover the truth, then praise God. If it is in His will that we must wait until Heaven to know the truth, then praise God.

I am content and safe in the knowledge of my eternal savior, Jesus Christ. He has never left or forsaken me, and he is with me right now.

"Vengence is mine, saith the Lord. I will repay." I do not have to worry about the Winston-Salem Police Department's version of truth and honesty, or justice. I am secure in God's hands.

Something a wise preacher, the late Pastor Curtis Whaley from Rosemont Baptist Church, told me is that "Men will let us down, but I have a God in heaven that will never let me down or disappoint me." I can depend on the Lord.

I have no desire to hurt anyone, even Willard Brown. He was a desperate man in a desperate situation. He must make his own peace and restitution with Almighty God. I forgive him. In addition, I hope that one day, Willard Brown will experience the love, salvation, and forgiveness that can only come from a personal relationship with the Lord Jesus Christ. I will pray for that for all people.

I wish he had been raised in a loving family like my own. We do not fight; we love and encourage each other. I praise my parents for the way they raised us; equal love for all five of us. We have come to know our parents as our best friends. I wish this kind of love for every family.

It is my prayer that all aspects of the Big Picture come together in God's time, and for God's purpose. If there is any small part I can play in bringing about His plan, then I will certainly participate in everyway possible.

Regina K. Lane and Dr. Linda F. Felker

CHAPTER SIX

Darryl Hunt Exonerated

Zechariah 8:16
These are the things you are to do: Speak the truth to each other, and render true and sound judgment in your courts

John 8:32
The truth shall set you free.

In order to understand the impact and significance of the Deborah Sykes rape and murder to my assault, it is critical that the events be outlined and the investigative methods used to solve the crime be analyzed.

In a highly publicized trial and re-trial, Darryl Hunt was convicted of Sykes' murder. Although he denied any involvement in the crime, he was convicted and spent 18 years of his life in prison.

DNA testing that was not available in the 80's was finally used in 2003 to prove that Willard Brown, not Darryl Hunt, had actually raped Deborah Sykes.

The murder of Sykes in 1984 polarized the City of Winston-Salem, and citizens were terrified that such an horrific act could take place.

Deborah Sykes, an employee of the Winston-Salem Sentinel Newspaper, was on her way to work on the morning of August 10, 1984. She never arrived.

She was kidnapped as she stepped out of her car to walk the short distance to the office. Deborah was assaulted and murdered in a field located adjacent to the Crystal Towers

Apartments in downtown Winston-Salem.

The Winston-Salem Police Department received a 911 call at 6:53 that morning, and the caller identified himself as Sammy Mitchell. (It was later discovered that the caller was not Sammy Mitchell, but Johnny Gray aka Johnny McConnell).

The caller reported that he witnessed an attack on a woman near the downtown fire station and Crystal Towers. The Police Communications Supervisor immediately dispatched officers to the scene; however, the police car was sent to the wrong location at Claremont and I-40.

The body of Deborah Sykes was found at approximately 1 p.m. that afternoon by a man who was passing by the field. I learned later that this man actually worked with my husband in the 1990's. The way his co-workers still tell the story, this man who found Deborah was walking. Realizing the police were searching for a woman's body, he just happened to be passing in that area at the time. This man was hauled into the police department, and questioned for many hours. He lived in fear for his own life.

Police began an intensive investigation into the crime, and the citizens of Winston-Salem were in shock. Many witnesses came forward, and indicated they either saw Deborah Sykes before she was attacked, witnessed the assault, saw the murder, or knew the identity of the men involved in killing her.

Darryl Hunt was named as a primary suspect in the crime from the first day, and detectives scoured the scene of the murder and surrounding areas in search of every scrap of evidence that could link Hunt to the crime.

Darryl Hunt was well known to police, and had experienced many run-ins with the law. He had been arrested multiple times during his 21 years, and had a history of violence.

While under investigation for the murder of Sykes, on September 8, 1984, Darryl Hunt shot a man in Winston-Salem. However, the victim did not immediately press charges. Instead, both Hunt and Sammy Mitchell were arrested for Disorderly Conduct and Resisting Arrest. The next day, the victim pressed charges against both men for the shooting.

A few days later, on September 11, police arrested Hunt for taking indecent liberties with a minor, referring to a sexual relationship he was having with a 15 year-old girl. This girl was Hunt's alibi for the morning of Deborah Sykes murder.

Witnesses to the attack on Deborah Sykes, living in the Crystal Towers Apartments, identified Darryl Hunt in a live police lineup on September 12, and again on September 13. That same day, an official charge of Indecent Liberties with a Minor Complaint was entered against Darryl Hunt.

On September 14, Hunt was charged with the murder of Deborah Sykes.

Thus began a long series of events that ultimately led to Darryl Hunt's conviction on the charge of First Degree Murder in the death of Deborah Sykes.

Hunt always proclaimed that he was innocent, and not involved in the Sykes case. His attorneys asserted that the physical evidence in the trial did not link Hunt to the rape or murder, and that eyewitnesses were unreliable. They also insisted that the other evidence gathered and presented at the trial was flimsy and inconsequential to the indictment.

However, Hunt was convicted and sentenced to prison for the crime. A series of appeals eventually led to a second trial for Hunt in 1989. The prosecution did a better job presenting the evidence the second time, and again, he was convicted of murdering Sykes.

Darryl had many supporters in the community, including prominent black religious leaders, and other political figures. The black community felt that the arrest and conviction was racially motivated. The city was divided along racial lines, and an undercurrent of distrust was prevalent in the city.

Hunt spent 18 years in prison for the crime, all the while insisting he did not kill Sykes. His defense attorneys lobbied for DNA testing of the physical evidence that was collected during the investigation. Even after Hunt's DNA did not match, people still assumed that he was there and participated in the assault and murder of Deborah Sykes.

Hunt's attorneys appealed his convictions to the North Carolina Supreme Court, and the Court upheld his conviction in 1994 and 1995. People always believed the police were right. They would not make a mistake of that magnitude. How could Darryl have been found guilty twice if he were not guilty.

In February 2000, the Fourth Circuit Court of Appeals upheld the federal district court's dismissal of Hunt's appeals, and in October of that same year, the United States Supreme Court denied Hunt's petition to review the 4th Circuit's decision.

My mother-in-law, Mary Lane, was the person who actually started the chain of events that led to Darryl Hunt's release from prison and eventual exoneration, although early on I tried very hard to convince detectives to make comparisons.

For years, Mrs. Lane felt that the police investigators had deliberately covered up the possibility of their conviction of an innocent man. After she met with Phoebe Zerwick, she thought I should come forward. In 2003, she was angry with me because I did not grant interviews with reporters from the local newspapers and media. I had to be in control of how my story was told.

I knew there are many truthful, hardworking police officers on the force! Mary Lane truly believed that the Winston-Salem Police Department was full of corruption and deceit, and she was angry that nothing was done to associate the evidence from my case to the Sykes case.

She wanted the police to help find evidence so I could see Willard Brown arrested and convicted for what he did to me. She believed that if Brown stood trial for his crime against me, it would force the Police Department to look again at the evidence in the Sykes case.

If Willard Brown was in prison when Deborah was murdered, how could he have committed both crimes?

I repeatedly told my Mother-in-Law, Mrs. Lane, that I did not believe the negative things she said about the police. I tried to convince her that they did what they could to help me at the time, and I refused to accept the possibility that my case was doomed from the start due to ineffective investigative methods. She did not work outside the home, and had plenty of time to talk on the phone, to read, and to think about the situation.

On February 2, 1985, my future mother-in-law was so upset over what happened to me, that she actually dreamed about the attack. In her dream, she saw Willard Brown wearing gloves that were fingerless, and the police were able to lift fingerprints from the crime scene to link him to the assault.

Of course, this was not the case. Brown was wearing grey gloves, and there were no fingerprints found. However, I am convinced that with today's DNA testing methods, positive identification could be made from skin particles found inside the glove.

That kind of DNA testing was not available in 1985. The glove was destroyed, along with all other physical evidence, in 1989.

Still, I believed that the police knew what they were doing, and I trusted them. Mrs. Lane did not trust the police and was strongly adamant that there was a cover-up involved in my case and in the Sykes case.

She formulated questions right after my attack, and insisted that I ask these questions of the detectives. I did ask the detectives her questions. She immediately made the connection between the cases, and was upset that Willard Brown was never arrested and charged for what he did to me.

In 2003, after seeing the articles run again, my mother-in-law contacted a reporter at the Winston-Salem Journal and told her about Willard Brown and my case. This reporter, Phoebe Zerwick, put her in contact with Mark Rabil, who is Darryl Hunt's defense attorney, and Richard McGough, Darryl's 1990 investigator.

Up until that day, Rabil did not know about Willard Brown or the circumstances of my case. This was appalling, especially because I had repeatedly informed the police of the possible connection between the two cases, and also because this information was not made available to Hunt's defense team during his trial. They might have known from newspaper articles about "The Integon Victim", but never made the association.

Of course, Mark Rabil made an immediate and logical connection between his client's situation and mine. Thus, the sequence of events began that would finally free Darryl Hunt.

My circumstances and the similarities between my case and the Sykes case were overwhelmingly clear, and Mark Rabil used this information to push for a complete exoneration for Darryl Hunt. Combined with the DNA testing that proved Hunt did not rape Sykes, it added positive proof that resulted in his release from prison. Even during this time, police and the Assistant District Attorney did not want me to talk with anyone. They said it could hurt the case and the investigation.

It is ironic to look back now, and know that my mother-in-law was the one to make the call to Phoebe Zerwick. The police say they solved the case with DNA evidence. At least the case is solved.

However, I know that Mary Lane solved the case and was responsible for the eventual exoneration of Darryl Hunt. They would not have had anything if Mary Lane had not come forward. The defense attorneys used the facts she provided to draw a line between the Sykes case and my case. It took many people to "never give up!" Mark Rabil had never heard of Willard Brown, and the police had told me years ago that our cases were not related.

My mother-in-law always believed the Crime Stoppers money would be paid to her for her assistance in solving this crime, but it never happened. She thought the cash reward would have at least been paid to her son Scott Lane and perhaps her daughter Vickie Lane on her behalf. But, of course, no reward was paid for the information she provided that solved the case.

The first time they ran his name through as a potential suspect, it did not draw a match, but surfaced Willard Brown's brother, Anthony Brown. However, the second time, Willard Brown's name appeared as the man I identified as my attacker and the DNA match. Finally, the connection was made after all those years.

If Mary Lane had not come forward a second time, it probably would have taken much longer for the police to identify Willard Brown.

I was hurt that my mother-in-law chose to go behind my back after all these years, and talk to the reporter and Mark Rabil. She should have told me, and asked me to go with her. She should have included me because it is my life, and the lives of my husband and children, that are impacted. What she did will have an impact on the rest of my life. It could have been a sweeter ending after all I had been through.

During the original investigation of my case in 1985, Mary Lane listened very intently. She insisted that I ask questions, and she believed from the start that there was a serial rapist on the loose in Winston-Salem. I did ask those questions.

We had many heated discussions about the way the detectives were handling, or not handling my complaint. I prefer to look at the positive side of situations, and I believe in the human goodness of people. Therefore, it was difficult for me to believe that there was a deliberate cover-up going on, and that the police were effectively neglecting my case in order to prosecute Darryl Hunt for the Sykes murder.

Actually, they sacrificed me for what they believed was a valid cause—the conviction of Darryl Hunt. Mary Lane knew this in her heart, and was furious about the circumstances. I had a hard time believing what she was saying, and tried to defend the detectives during each conversation with her. I revisited this in 1986—1989, during the re-investigation, and in 2006 with the Sykes Administrative Review Committee.

In the end, Mary was right. She was right about the cover-up; she was right about Willard Brown. I guess in my heart I knew she was right, but it was so hard for me to accept the hard facts before me because I was told differently by the police department. I still thought it was the police department's job to solve this. Lifetime Movies prove over and over again that victims and their families can help solve criminal cases for and with law enforcement. But for me, real life was not like a Lifetime Movie.

At the time, I could only wonder what would make Phoebe call and ask me questions. After 18 years, Phoebe learned by phone that I had been convinced that my case had nothing to do with Deborah's case, and she quoted this in the newspaper.

It was my hope that it was going to be like the movies, the cops always get the bad guys. It did not happen that way.

Mary Lane was interviewed by the Winston-Salem Journal, and they published the "On a Hunch" article in January 2004. This further solidified the information needed to set Darryl Hunt free.

My mother-in-law was diagnosed with cancer, and died in the spring of 2004. She did not live to see the full outcome of this case, or the results of the Sykes Administrative Review Committee. She did not live to realize her hope that there would be full disclosure and accountability for the Sykes murder and my attack by Willard Brown.

I wish she had lived to see these things happen, for it would have given her great comfort, and possibly eased her own suffering to know that I would finally have my day. What she did brought closure for many people!

I enjoyed talking with Mary. She could be very girdy and strong-willed. She had strong opinions of the police and their handling of the cases. She would sometimes get mad if I did not see things her way. She loved to talk about her love and her hate for the politicians.

My hope was to talk more to her about my loving Lord that saw me through a very difficult time—a time of fear, sadness, many emotions, and much gratefulness.

This was the last thing she proved before she died. I know that many people are forever grateful, especially Darryl and April Hunt.

So, in the end, my mother-in-law provided the missing pieces in November 2003 when she talked to Phoebe

Zerwick, Richard McGough, and Mark Rabil. She told them about me, my ordeal, and gave them Willard Brown's name. Finally, advances in DNA testing identified Willard Brown as the rapist of Deborah Sykes, and Darryl Hunt was exonerated.

Willard Brown. The same man whom I believed had kidnapped, raped, robbed, and stabbed me. The same man I identified in a photo lineup and in a live, in-person lineup.

There were so many errors and multiple inconsistencies during the Sykes investigation. Some of the witnesses were not credible, and evidence was not substantial. The best and most logical course of investigation should have started with connecting any possible links to other similar crimes.

There were four potentially related attacks in the downtown Winston-Salem area during an eight-month period of time beginning in June 1984, and ending with the attack of me on February 2, 1985. I still believe there could be more, not just in Winston-Salem, but also in other nearby towns and cities, if Willard Brown lived in other cities like Thomasville or High Point.

The similarities of these four cases are undeniable; yet detectives chose to pursue charges against Darryl Hunt and ignore the connection to the other rapes.

Yet, through it all, *God was in control.* We may never understand why the sequence of events happened the way they did. At least not on this earth. Nevertheless, there will be a day of reckoning, when God will put all things right.

In His Word, God says, *"For the Lamb, which is in the midst of the Throne, shall feed them, and shall lead them into living fountains of water, and God shall wipe away all tears from their eyes."* Revelation 7:17

This is such a precious promise to me, for it means that regardless of what I experience in this earthly body, God will make things right. God will also make all things right for others, if they put their trust in Jesus Christ.

"For he has set a day when he will judge the world with justice…" Acts 17:31.

God also commands us to be merciful to others. *"For in the same way you judge others, you will be judged, and with the measure you use, it will be measured to you." Matthew 7:2*

This instruction from the Word of God helps me to cope with the injustice that I have had through the legal system. *"God will judge men's secrets through Jesus Christ." Romans 2:16.*

There are so many precious promises in God's word that have given me comfort and strength for the past 22 years. It is my heart's desire that everyone involved in the false conviction of Darryl Hunt for the rape of Deborah Sykes be judged mercifully.

It is possible that the series of events, and the consequences of the botched investigation, were simply mistakes, and not intentional. I will not try to judge their hearts, or their actions. It is not my place to judge; it is my place to inform.

The Bible has taught me that I will not get into Heaven by the works that I do. Salvation's plan is so simple; understand that we are all sinners. Christ died on a cruel cross to save us from our sins. All we have to do is ask for forgiveness for our sins, accept His free gift, and believe in the Lord Jesus, and we will be saved. Years after I accepted Christ as my Savior, I followed the Lord in baptism.

God's timetable is not man's timetable, and I remind myself of that fact everyday. I always want to be in His will, and I never felt it was God's will for me to allow my identity to be revealed until now. The police protected my identity.

Ecclesiastis 3:1-8. To every thing there is a season, and a time to every purpose under the Heaven. A time to be born, and a time to die; a time to plant and a time to pluck up that which is planted. A time to kill, and a time to heal; a time to break down, and a time to build up. A time to weep, and a time to laugh; a time to mourn, and a time to dance. A time to cast away stones, and a time to gather stones together; a time to embrace, and a time to refrain from embracing. A time to eat, and a time to lose; a time to keep, and a time to cast away. A time to rend, and a time to sew; a time to keep silent, and a time to speak. A time to love, and a time to hate; a time of war, and a time of peace ."

Throughout each decision and every situation, I have tried to maintain a willing and obedient attitude, and exhibited patience—a lot of patience! I want to do the right thing at the right time.

I rejoice that Darryl Hunt was finally exonerated of the rape of Deborah Sykes without prejudice. He can never be tried for this crime again. I do not know anyone that likes to be blamed for something they did not do. Although there are many people in the community that believe he was involved in some way with the abduction and murder of Sykes, as the judge said, we know for certain that he did not rape her. That alone is evidence enough to create doubt that he was in anyway involved.

Knowing and seeing the information provided to me, I know that Willard Brown was indeed our attacker. Witnesses in the case for Darryl were not always honest. It feels like we have been brainwashed.

The technical terminology for this is **Cognitive Dissonance.** A simple definition of this phrase is to alter someone's knowledge by use of emotional blackmail. It creates uncomfortable tension that comes from holding two conflicting thoughts at the same time. Knowledge serves as the driving force that compels the mind to invent a new belief, or alter an existing believe.

Cognitive Dissonance is the mind controller's best friend. It is used to control others, even when the evidence seems to be against them. With this kind of irrational thinking, people are forced to trust a perceived authority. People do not arrive at their irrational beliefs overnight. They come to their conclusion over a period of time by being continually influenced or provided with false information. A mental conflict occurs when that information creates a contradictory situation.

Cognitive Dissonance is a very powerful motivator that will lead people to change their beliefs. It creates a state of confusion when facts are twisted into half-truths, and collide with common sense. This is the power of Cognitive Dissonance. It can change fact into fiction because of the emotions involved. It is like discovering that a trusted friend is really untrustworthy and has been manipulating you all along.

Fear rules. *Truth* is the first casualty of this tactic, and is followed by getting rid of information contrary to the belief they want to instill in you.

Therefore, in our minds we hear Deborah Sykes' name, and automatically see Darryl Hunt's face. Brown's face is the one that needs to appear in our minds.

I too believed that Darryl was guilty based on what I had been told by the Police Department over the years and by what was reported in the Winston-Salem Journal. It was not until talking with Lt. Joseph Ferrelli on February 3, 2006, that I continued to believe in the sincerity of his and the staff's work.

Lt. Ferrelli told me before that he was on the streets back in 1984—1986. His wife did not work far from where I was abducted. He said if he had known a killer was still on the streets, that he would have taken extra precautions to protect his wife. He said, "We didn't know."

We are still learning, and I am confident that I can trust the information provided by the Sykes Administrative Review Committee findings.

I am so very disappointed that the investigational information used by the 1980's detectives could not be discussed by them. What were they thinking? Why couldn't they go back to see if there were other attacks? Why couldn't they consider an attacker (mine and Deborah's), to be shorter than 6 foot tall, considering the abduction from the building. Why couldn't they consider those things, even though I was at least five inches shorter than Deborah and about 15 pounds lighter. My attacker seemed to be under the influence of alcohol or other substances.

My Heavenly Father gave me the courage and confidence to react.

Think about heaven. Revelations 21 tells us that we become a new person when we die. Darryl Hunt is a different person today than he was in 1985. God takes the old person we are, and through His saving grace, makes us new. Just like the seasons on earth that change—spring, summer, winter, and fall.

My reason for coming forward at this point in my life is to help clarify what I was feeling and thinking. I know people care. I have seen it in the reaction of people who know my story today.

As I told the Sykes Administrative Review Committee on February 2, 2006, I have come here not to be part of the problem, but part of the solution. I hope something I have said here will help others see how they can help themselves and help others, and to sincerely help to improve the process.

I think it is important to communicate, and keep everyone, including the victims and their families, updated during the process.

Police should be required to review cases with the victims, especially if detectives change, and addendums should be written to further document the details of the case.

There should be satisfaction surveys for victims. I still wonder why Detective Crump did not return to Brown with an attorney in 1986.

To date, no one has thoroughly reviewed my case; a partial review was done with Detective Rowe, but there were no addendums.

I want to thank Mark Rabil and Darryl Hunt for visiting my mother-in-law, and sister-in-law Vickie Lane, in Forsyth Hospital before she passed away. I look for them and the people around them to do great things that will benefit many citizens.

I am glad that my time has come, and that, at last, I am able to step forward with full disclosure of the police investigation of my case. I believe that 100% disclosure will not be given until everyone talks, including the retired detectives.

Regina K. Lane and Dr. Linda F. Felker

CHAPTER SEVEN

Willard Brown's Confession

Galatians 6:7-8
Be not deceived; God is not mocked: for whatsoever a man soweth, that shall he also reap. For he that soweth to his flesh shall of the flesh reap corruption; but he that soweth to the Spirit shall of the Spirit reap life everlasting.

On December 19, 2003, I learned from a Winston-Salem detective, Mike Rowe, and an SBI agent, Scott Williams, that the person I picked from a lineup in 1986, Willard Brown, was the same person that had also raped and killed newspaper editor, Deborah Sykes.

I still have to laugh about a friend and co-worker, Sue Conrad filling in as receptionist that day. After the detective and the SBI agent left, she said, "Regina, they said they needed to talk with you. I insisted that you were busy and working." Still, three years later, she has no idea who she was trying to get rid of. Detective Rowe told me she was tough. I told her that was okay. Yes, today, she knows the truth.

Earl Wall, the senior attorney and friend from work, came into the conference room on the first floor of our office building, and was with me that day when they came to tell me that it was Willard Brown. I thought my knees were going to buckle under me from the shock of things *(and they still may one day)*. Earl was my comfort and support, and had worked with me at Integon. In 2003, we had known each other for eighteen years, like many other people I work with today.

They told me the same person that I picked out in a lineup years ago was the same person that matched the DNA evidence collected in the Deborah Sykes rape and murder. I remembered that I had asked the officials to conduct any and every test in the beginning.

According to police documents, and newspaper accounts, investigators said that they began looking at Willard Brown as a suspect in the case because he had been identified as a suspect in the Integon rape six months after Deborah Sykes was murdered.

As I stated before, Mary Lane, my mother-in-law, was largely responsible today for Willard Brown being identified today as a possible connection to the Sykes murder case. She talked to a newspaper reporter Phoebe Zerwick and Mark Rabil, Hunt's defense attorney in 2003. She told them that I had identified Willard Brown as my assailant, and provided details of the assault.

They were amazed, and did not know that I identified Brown years ago. In fact, Brown's name never came up at all during the years Hunt was imprisoned.

Now, they had a possible connection. After DNA taken from Sykes during the original investigation was found to match with Brown's DNA, he confessed to the crime on December 19, 2003, and said that he acted alone. This went against the eyewitness accounts of the attack, which asserted that there were two or three men involved in the attack. People believe there was more than one. Maybe three—five black men were around Deborah that day.

A simple explanation of DNA is that is the chromosomal chemical components of genetic information. In other words, each individual has a twisted ladder of molecular structure that is unlike anyone else's. In fact, each person has over three billion base pairs of combinations. This is why a positive match of DNA chromosomes is nearly 100% accurate.

DNA resides in the chromosomes located in the genetic cells. Almost all cells in the human body contain 23 pairs of chromosomes. DNA can be extracted from virtually any part of the human body. The most common source of DNA is blood or soft tissue samples. DNA can also be extracted from semen, saliva, hair, and even skin cells.

Two factors affect the accuracy of DNA testing: the number of genetic loci tested and their nature. More than 99% of DNA is identical between all people, and if it were analyzed, there would be no difference found between two individuals. However, there is a certain area of DNA that is unique for every individual. Testing the 16 STR lock for DNA samples gives a probability of 99.9999% accuracy.

Thus, when in a criminal case, DNA samples are said to match, there is almost 100% certainty, and that is the reason courts allow DNA tests as evidence.

Therefore, based on the DNA match between Sykes and Brown, the Winston-Salem Police charged Willard E. Brown in connection with a string of crimes involving the 1984 death of Deborah Sykes. A Forsyth County Grand Jury formally indicted Brown in February 2004 on the same charges, and the case moved to Forsyth Superior Court.

A grand jury is different that a trial jury that deliberates and decides the guilt or innocence of the defendant. A grand jury only hears evidence from the investigator's side of the case, and determines if there is sufficient evidence to move forward to court.

Sykes' DNA was tested with Darryl Hunt's in 1994 and 1995, and there was not a positive match. Instead, the DNA testing was inconclusive. He was not granted a new trial. The courts stated that the DNA evidence alone did not rule him out as being the killer or having participated in her assault.

Darryl Hunt spent 18 years in prison for Sykes' death. He was officially cleared of these charges on Friday, February 6, 2004. Judge Anderson Cromer said that there was no evidence connecting Hunt with Willard Brown. Hunt was exonerated weeks after DNA testing led to the arrest of Willard Brown.

In December 2004, I was present in the courtroom with my mother and the Sykes family when Willard Brown was sentenced to prison for the murder of Deborah Sykes. This was part of the closure for me. It was a great relief to know that Brown was off the streets and could not hurt another woman.

I was happy that my mother was able to get away from the family business and go with me to court that day. She stopped by to pick me up, and I walked around to the passenger side of the car to get in; however, my mother was already seated there and asked me to drive. She startled me, and I jumped back in fear; then, we both laughed hysterically! She handed me a pad and a pen and said, "You might need this." She is always so thoughtful.

We arrived at the courthouse about 10:30 a.m. and rode up the elevator to the DA's office. As the door opened, I looked to the right to see many people congregated, and looked to the left toward the DA's office to see the familiar, smiling face of Detective Mike Rowe. He motioned with his hand for us to walk his way.

As we approached him at the District Attorney's door, I introduced my mother and we went inside. I introduced my mother to SBI Agent Scott Williams, and Assistant DA Eric Saunders.

Eric asked my mother and me to follow him, and led us down a hallway into another room. There, we met Mrs. Evelyn Jefferson, Deborah Sykes mother, and several members of her family.

Mrs. Jefferson and I hugged, and were so glad to finally meet. Eric told us that Willard Brown would be brought into the courtroom at 11:00 a.m. Mrs. Jefferson then introduced my mother and me to her family. I feel so badly for the way Deborah's family suffered. We began talking, and sharing experiences. Mrs. Jefferson asked if I still had physical scars from my attack, and I said yes, and began showing them my scars and telling them what had happened to me.

Everyone in the room was very compassionate towards me, and listened intently to what I was saying. Then, the door opened again, and Eric said it was time to go to the courtroom. My mother's cheeks were red, and I had seen that look before. I asked her if she was OK, and she said yes. I knew this was a day bringing back terrible memories for her, reliving the day that she and my father met me at the hospital to find my spirit broken and my body bleeding. They sat in the room with Detective Miller when I gave an account of what happened.

We filed out of the room, me, my mother, Mrs. Jefferson and her family, Eric Saunders, Tom Keith, Mike Rowe, and Scott Williams. Before we reached the courtroom, I turned one more time to check on my mother. She said, "I feel so guilty." We all stopped, and Mrs. Jefferson so graciously consoled my mother. She asked her why she felt guilty and my mother said, "Because I have my daughter here and you do not have your daughter here."

Mrs. Jefferson embraced my mother and told her please do not ever feel guilty' just be thankful that you do have her here. They embraced, and we all regained our composure and then proceeded to the courtroom.

We filed into the courtroom through a doorway behind the judge's bench on the right side of the room. We were seated on the third row, with Mrs. Jefferson's family entering first, then my mother, then me and finally Mrs. Jefferson.

I knew that there would be many Darryl Hunt supporters in the courtroom, including his father-in-law and Mark Rabil.

Willard Brown's family was already in the room, seated on the far end of the second bench. As the bailiffs escorted Willard Brown into the courtroom from a doorway behind the judge's bench to the left, Brown spoke to a family member. The bailiff asked him to be quiet.

I remember that as we sat together, Mrs. Jefferson and I continued talking and asking questions about how I was treated by the police. It was like two best friends sitting there, trying to catch up on many things in a short amount of time. One question Mrs. Jefferson asked me was if I had asked the police to compare cases, and I told her yes. I explained that within the first five days into the investigation of my attack, I had asked the detectives and investigators to compare my case with Deborah's case.

My heart was racing as the court session began. Eric

Saunders said a few words, and Willard Brown was supposed to swear on the Bible to tell the truth; however, he refused. The judge asked him many questions. Brown would hesitate, answer yes, but shake his head no at the same time.

Pete Clary, Willard Brown's court-appointed defense attorney, gave an account of the last part of Deborah's life. Mrs. Jefferson leaned forward, and we all strained to hear every word he spoke. The whole scenario unfolding before us seemed much orchestrated, as they had planned and practiced what would be said, and how it would be said.

Clary gave an account of Willard Brown as to what had actually happened to Deborah and how she died, per Willard Brown. He told the court that Willard Brown had been in and out of prison since the age of ten. He was handicapped in school, and was one of sixteen children. His sister, Brenda, was murdered in 1990. His mother, now deceased, was alive in 1984. He had two friends his whole life, and one of them was Michael Thomas.

Clary stated that Brown weighted 125 to 130 pounds and was 24 years old at the time of Sykes murder. Brown had gotten out of prison in June before the murder in August. That day and the night before, he was celebrating his birthday. He had liquor and other substances.

Brown was at the scene at 6:30 a.m. to 7 a.m. that morning of August 10, 1984, and he was alone. It was just going to be a robbery. He had his hand in his pocket, and told Deborah to go with him. Flashbacks began in my own mind as I remembered again being taken away at gunpoint.

Clary said they walked toward the park near Crystal Towers. Deborah did not have much money with her; in fact, she only had change.

He told her to take her pants off and she only pulled them halfway down. The flashbacks continued as I was also made to undress at gunpoint in front of this stranger.

He opened his pocketknife and laid it on the ground. I was frustrated as I listened to this account and took notes. Deborah would not have willingly had sex with Brown. Learning from her family that she was a Christian woman, I am sure she fought just as I did!

Brown was having sex with Deborah when he thought he heard someone in the bushes. He saw two legs. Then, Deborah started hitting Brown, and that is when he killed her. He ran when he saw someone, and supposedly went to his mother's house. Deborah's pants were found 20 feet away from her body, on the other side of the fence. We still wonder if Brown entered the Hyatt House to wash himself before going to his mother's home.

Clary then asked for life with no parole based on the 1984 sentencing law; then he had to correct himself. He said first-degree sentence should be life plus ten years.

During this time, Brown turned around looking at us, glaring at us with his eyes. The newspaper photographer took a picture of Mr. Brown and his glare. The bailiff made him turn back around, and another bailiff walked around the courtroom, keeping an eye on everyone.

Judge Todd Burke sentenced Willard Brown to life in prison plus ten years. This actually means 21 years and 3 months. The perspective of this sentence is so wrong. He would not serve life in prison. I knew that Judge Burke was a very good judge, as I had sat on a jury under his supervision. I had confidence in him.

I had been told that he would be locked up until he was 70 years old. Now, in the courtroom, I realized what the Winston-Salem Journal reported was true: he would only be locked up until he was 65 years old. Those five years were significant to me. He would be back on the streets, and able to hurt somebody else at age 65.

Court was dismissed. I was standing behind Mrs. Jefferson when a newspaper photographer took our picture, which was published in the Winston-Salem Journal the next day. We filed out of the third row, and went back into the conference room behind the courtroom and waited for the press and others to leave. Mrs. Jefferson, her family, my mother, and I continued to share our stories.

Mrs. Jefferson and her family described what court was like for them during Deborah's first and second trials. They felt terrorized by men in the courtroom. Stares with evil eyes and men raking their fingers across their own necks to imitate knives cutting their throats were common examples of this intimidation. Deborah Sykes' family were told that they were "next" by these men. The DA told them there could not be any outbursts of emotions or they would be escorted from the courtroom. I cannot imagine what that was like for them!

I praise God for giving them strength and courage to face this difficult situation in their lives.

On December 20, 2004, Phoebe called and asked how I survived the attack, what happened during the investigation, how I identified Brown, and why I decided not to prosecute. She told me the panel draws heavily on newspaper articles. Phoebe was trying to tell me that public officials react when they see things in the paper. She was talking about changes that she thought were good, and reforms like the Innocence Group.

She talked about the Attorney General, the Commission, the head of the SBI, university law professors, chief justices, and other political figures. She asked me if Mrs. Jefferson was disappointed and if she still thought that Darryl Hunt was guilty. I told Phoebe that I could not answer for Mrs. Jefferson.

Phoebe told me she was going to get a copy of my police report. I was so surprised, because I had not been able to get it. She said she would call me when and if she was able to obtain a copy, and she did. It took me 21 years and one day to get my report.

Since then, I have declined many requests for an interview for articles in the Winston-Salem Journal. I did not want to say anything that would hurt the people who had endured too much pain already. I wanted the system to work before I shared my feelings and opinions.

I have met and interviewed with police personnel to clarify details about my story. After making my presentation to the Sykes Administrative Review Committee, I also met and interviewed with Mark Rabil, the defense attorney for Darryl Hunt, and his investigator, Richard McGough. Mark was a persistent man, seeking the truth and justice. Richard was also persistent, and called me frequently. He is a very empathetic, compassionate man. Both are dedicated to making right the things that went so wrong. They patiently waited for two years for me to open up and tell my story.

There have been many newspaper articles published questioning how police could have missed the connection between the four cases. I asked Bill Miller if there were other crimes like mine in 1985, when he was the lead detective on my case. He told me no, not that he knew of, but other detectives might be working on some. His statement clearly misled me. According to police records, at the same time Miller was investigating my case, he was also investigating the Sykes case.

Investigative reports from my rape in 1985 clearly show many similarities to the rape and murder of Deborah Sykes. The articles also reported that I had identified Brown as my attacker. Most astonishingly are the two pictures: one of Deborah and one of me, both taken after our attacks. Just as police attorney, Julie Risher, Lieutenant Joe Ferrelli, and Sargeant Chuck Bryom told me as I looked at the pictures with them in the Public Safety Center in October 2006, the injuries were the same.

I give an open invitation for police personnel to talk with me. I am ready to listen. There are many questions that I need answered, and the City of Winston-Salem deserves to understand what went wrong in all four of the rape investigations. There are so many startling omissions from my documented police report, and the obvious connection between my case and Sykes case was either overlooked or ignored.

Some interesting facts include:

• The Winston-Salem City Manager requested a 2nd investigation into the Deborah Sykes case in early 1985 due to what he considered "shoddy police work in the first investigation." That investigation was going on, and coincided with, the investigation of my kidnapping and rape in 1985.

• According to police records, my 1985 rape investigation case was closed and all the evidence was destroyed in September 1989, just four months after the North Carolina Supreme court ordered a second trial for Hunt. This coincided with the police investigating the Deborah Sykes case for the third time. My case was investigated when it happened. A year and one month later, Brown was found and brought in for questioning. I was also brought back in for questions in 1989, before Darryl went to trial.

• Police interviewed Willard Brown in March 1986 in connection with the Sykes murder, but the report written about that interview makes no mention of the evidence the police had gathered against Brown in my 1985 rape. In addition, this report was never turned over to defense attorneys and was not released publicly until January 2004.

• Even the SBI agents and police officers, whose job it was to re-investigate the Sykes case, did not pursue the connection. If Hunt's defense team had known about Willard Brown and my case in 1993, they could have had DNA tests done that would have identified Brown. Hunt would have been free at least ten years earlier.

• Tom Keith, District Attorney, said in February 2004 "just knowing how law enforcement works and how myopic we get, I just think that's the way things work out sometimes." *(The word myopic means narrow-minded. It appears he was saying that the police investigation was narrow-minded. If so, the explanation is atrocious when compared to the lives involved!).*

• The detectives and investigators involved in my case were also involved at times in the Sykes murder investigation. These include my first lead detective Bill Miller, Carter Crump, R.C. Spoon, Teresa Hicks, Randy Weavil, G.C. Cornatzer, and Mike McCoy.

• None of the police reports in my case mention any possibility of similarities between my case and the Sykes case. Surely, some of these detectives had to draw a connection. *(This is especially true given the fact that Miller, Crump, and I talked about Deborah's case every time we spoke!)* Any good homicide cop would make the connection.

• The similarities between the two crimes were the primary reason that Tom Keith motioned to vacate the murder conviction against Darryl Hunt. Willard Brown said that he acted alone, and Keith pointed out similarities between the Sykes rape and murder to "The Integon" rape and assault and attempted murder. He stated, *"There is no question there is only one assailant"* in my case.

• Carter Crump, the second detective who was assigned to my case, said that he did connect the two crimes, but that he checked prison records and thought Brown was in jail on the day Sykes was killed. I wonder how these facts are documented today?

• Crump stated, "If I've got two similar cases going on two blocks away, don't you think I would have followed up until I find out that he was in jail? That is what I did. If I didn't document it, that's an error on my part."

• There is no certainty of when the police actually checked Brown's prison record, and there is no documentation in my police report that discloses Brown's prison record.

• Detective Crump interviewed Willard Brown in March 1986 in connection with the Sykes case. He denied any role in the crime. However, Crump's report does not mention that Brown was a suspect in my case. Keep in mind that this was the same time that I identified Brown in a live police lineup. Crump stated that he did not remember why he left those details out of the report.

• Mark Rabil believed that prosecutors withheld information that could have helped in Hunt's defense. He thought the police reports were carefully written by the police in such a way that any prosecutor or judge who might be reading the report would conclude that it was not something that had to be turned over to the defense attorney as exculpatory. I know personally from Eric Saunders, Detective Mike Rowe, and SBI Scott Williams that my case is the discovery evidence in the case for Deborah Sykes against Willard Brown.

Is it possible that the police would do that in order to hide the connection between Deborah Sykes's case and my case?

Only God knows the true intent of people's hearts. *Jeremiah 16:17: "My eyes are on all their ways; they are not hidden from me, nor is their sin concealed from my eyes."*

I believe there will be an accounting day, and God will reveal the full truth of what happened, who was involved, and if there was a deliberate cover-up.

Psalms 44:21: "Shall not God search this out? For He knoweth the secrets of the heart."

1 Corinthians 14:25: "And the secrets of the heart will be laid bare..."

Isaiah 3:9: "The look on their faces testifies against them...they flaunt their sin. They do not conceal it. Woe to them, for they have brought evil on themselves."

CHAPTER EIGHT

Sykes Administrative Review Committee

Deuteronomy 13:12-15
If you hear it said about one of the towns...that wicked men have arisen among you and have led the people of their town astray, ...then you must inquire, probe and investigate it thoroughly, if it is true and it has been proved that this detestable thing has been done among you.

I need to know the truth of why my case was put on the back burner and never taken seriously. According to the Committee findings, the official police report detailing my case was written on February 5, 1985, and was incorrect.

I feel that I was overlooked and never taken seriously. I did my best to make sure the investigators had all the information they needed to solve the crime; however, 22 years later, the official police report is still incorrect and Brown has not been brought to justice for what he did to me. I chose not to prosecute.

It was my hope that it was going to be like the movies, the cops always get the bad guys. It did not happen that way. This is a storm that has thundered, rained, and poured on me for 27 years.

I do not like to say bad things about people. I prefer to look at the positive things and find the good side of people. But, it has been difficult because of what happened to me and others, and how the cases were handled from the start.

They simply would not listen to what I was telling them, both the actual details and facts of the attack, and the possible connection of Willard Brown to other attacks in the city.

Mark Rabil first talked with me on January 19, 2004. It took two years *(December 2003 to February 19, 2006)* for me to talk with Mark Rabil and Richard McGough after I realized what was going on. They were very patient, waiting for the time when I felt comfortable to talk to them. Now, we eagerly awaited the results of the Committee's investigation of how the police handled the Deborah Sykes murder case, plus information on how they handled my case and the other two rape cases.

Mrs. Jefferson, Deborah Sykes' mother, needs to know the truth of what happened. I need to know the truth of what happened. The other victims and their families need to know what happened. The citizens of Winston-Salem deserve to know the truth.

The Sykes Administrative Review Committee was created to take a thorough look at the actions of the police investigators and detectives during the Deborah Sykes investigation. They also reviewed all related crimes during that same period of time, and realized that the review would go much deeper than originally intended.

This was not just about the Sykes case, but included my case and two other rape cases as well.

The first meeting of the Committee was July 26, 2005, and continued to meet monthly thereafter. The scope of their research and investigation included a list of concerns and operating guidelines:

• Review police actions in these cases, and caution against making snap judgments or drawing premature conclusions

• Receive cooperation from the District Attorney's office to help find the truth, and seek cooperation from all other parties involved in these cases

• Alleviate community concerns and ensure that positive changes prevent this from happening again

• Promote positive changes in the police department

In addition, the Committee proposed to seek answers to these, and other questions and concerns:

• Understand the parameters used in putting together similar events

• Investigate how the Regina K. investigation was handled the first time Willard Brown was identified as a suspect

• Understand how potential crimes are linked now as opposed to 1984

• Review procedures for retaining physical evidence now as opposed to then

• Identify what changes in process have been implemented

A list of potential interviewees was compiled, and requests were sent to these individuals asking them to provide testimony and/or conduct interviews in order to document their association and involvement in any of the rape cases.

Some people declined to be interviewed, and cited a variety of reasons why they did not want to be involved in the actions of the Committee. However, a large number of people willingly accepted the opportunity to speak, and provided insight and details to the investigations of these cases.

Some people were interviewed by telephone and their statements presented in written format to the Committee. Others agreed to appear in person before the Committee and provide their testimony and answer questions.

Among the individuals who declined to participate were many of the detectives and investigators who were involved in the Sykes case and in my case.

Others sent their statements in writing for Committee Review. Benjamin Dowling-Sendor, the Assistant Appellate Defender, wrote a lengthy letter to the Committee. He was one of Darryl Hunt's attorneys, and began working on Hunt's case in 1992.

In his letter, he remarked that he was troubled by the facts of my case in comparison to the Sykes case, and that the defense team was not made aware of the possible connection. He pointed out the obvious similarities, two white women, both abducted in downtown Winston-Salem early in the morning just after leaving our cars on our way to work. Both victims were stabbed with a knife, both victims were robbed, and both victims were raped. He said that the Integon victim was eager to help police find her assailant and it seemed very odd that my case would be suddenly dropped.

He wanted the Committee to answer questions as to why I dropped the case, were the same officers involved in investigating both cases, and why they did not pursue the connection between our cases.

Mark Rabil spoke to the Committee in December 2005. He began his remarks by talking about the Integon rape case *(MY CASE!)*, which he considered to be significant in terms of its relation to the Sykes rape and murder. Rabil asked why disclosures were not made to the Darryl Hunt defense team.

There were a large number of officers involved in the investigation of both cases, and "the Integon victim" was very cooperative; however, there is no reference to Willard Brown being interviewed for the crime even after he was identified. Mr. Rabil asserted that the details of the Integon case were carefully left out of the report so that the Hunt defense team would not make a connection.

Willard Brown was arrested on other charges in 1986, and the Integon victim picked Brown from a police lineup at that time. Rabil said he found it very strange that I declined to pursue my case any further when I had been so cooperative and available for months, and aggressively worked with investigators to apprehend Brown. Rabil also acknowledged that the defense team would never have known about Willard Brown if my mother-in-law had not disclosed the information.

James Allen, the Director of Security at the Integon Building when I was attacked, was interviewed by the Committee. He stated that, even though many questions were raised at the time, the detectives refused to go there with their investigation. There was a closed mindset that could not be penetrated. The police were right; everyone else was wrong.

On January 6, 2006, Lieutenant Ferrelli called and said that he and Sargeant Byrom were assisting the City Manager and the review committee. They were looking at other cases related to Deborah Sykes, and wanted to interview me at the police department or wherever I preferred.

They were concerned that, in my case, I identified Willard Brown, but explained that I was not the primary focus. Lieutenant Ferrelli told me that he did not want to drudge up the past, but wanted to know if they did everything they could do to help me at the time.

They were looking at internal affairs and police procedures. I asked him if there was a list of questions, and he said no. I asked if anyone else had testified, and he said that I would be the first. I asked how many victims, and he said four. I told him that I did not want anyone else speaking on my behalf.

I continued asking a multitude of questions to make sure I fully understood the procedures and intent. I asked him if my testimony would be on video or tape recording, and if this was considered a deposition. He said he did not know. I asked if there was a civil suit under consideration, and he said he did not know. I asked who was going to listen to this, and he said it would be public record. I asked if I could get a signed statement that my name would not be released to the media. Lieutenant Ferrelli told me that the media would get the final report from the Committee. He explained that Chief Norris said this was a new procedure, and that my police report could not be released.

On January 12, 2006, I called Lieutenant Ferrelli and asked if he could provide me with a list of the basic questions he would ask me during the interview. He said they were questions in his head, and not on paper. He explained that each of my answers would be the deciding factor of the next question from him.

He told me that my case was re-opened several times in the late 1980's. I was still trying to get my police report released to me. I did not want anybody else in my life to speak for me, possibly shorten my statement, leave something out, or misrepresent the facts.

We spoke again the next day, and he told me about the four cases that were under review. He said the cases were all similar, and that in each of the cases a black man raped a white woman. He talked about the similarities of date, time, location, and scope of the investigation, and explained that the duty of the city council was to determine if these cases were actually related.

He said he did not know about any civil litigation, and that the committee was only addressing police procedures. They were not looking at the cases in the realm of police conduct. They tried to give me an overview of as many related facts as possible. Basically, he said they were trying to determine why the comparisons were not made at the time.

I decided to meet with the committee and provide my statement in person at a public forum. It was the right thing to do, and the right time in my life to step forward.

I wanted to talk to the man who saved my life, and I called Mr. Wagner on January 23, 2006. He confirmed to me that after my attack on February 2, 1985, no one ever returned to talk to him. He did recall that a reporter, Phoebe Zerwick, spoke to him a couple of years ago and said she was writing an article, but that he never saw an article published in the newspaper. Phoebe gave me Mr. Wagner's phone number.

I just broke down and cried that day. Mr. Wagner was so sweet and patient with me, saying, *"Go ahead honey, just take your time and get it out, let your tears fall."* Mr. Wagner said he had all the time in the world if I needed to talk to him. What an extraordinary man!

I asked Mr. Wagner to go with me to the Committee meeting so he could be there when I made my statement on February 2, 2006, and he agreed. He made a big impact, and I was pleased to introduce him to the Committee that evening as the man who saved my life.

When the investigations started again, I felt connected by the memories but felt like I was looking into the life of another person...even though it was me.

The two weekends before I spoke to the Committee, I spent time in prayer and scripting my comments. I wanted to include all relevant facts, and answer any questions. I told Chief Norris and Lieutenant Ferrelli before February 2, 2006, that I had invited Mark Rabil and Richard McGough to the Committee meeting to hear my statement. They asked me why I invited them, and I told them we are all pieces of the puzzle. We must have each piece in order to see the whole picture.

I was impressed with Lieutenant Ferrelli when I tried to explain to him that Mr. Wagner was with me, my unsung hero. Lieutenant Ferrelli stopped me and said, *"I appreciate you telling me, but you don't have to. You go and make your statement and say whatever you need to. It's okay."* It was a breath of freedom, reassuring to me, permitting me, to do that.

Lieutenant Ferrelli took me in the back room when I arrived that evening. When I testified before the committee on February 2, 2006, I addressed as many questions about my case and the connection to the Sykes case as possible, knowing that people wanted to know the specifics of what happened.

These were actually questions presented to me by Mark Rabil and Richard McGough on January 12, 2004. I thought if I answered these questions, that it would answer most people's questions. It did.

As I gave my statement to the committee, I tried to say good things about the detectives. At the time, in 1985 and 1986, I felt like they were my big brothers, walking by my side. Looking back, I remember that they appeared to try to comfort me. Now I question their true motives. Were they really trying to help me, or were they simply pacifying me in order to move forward with their other, more important cases?

After I spoke, everyone looked at each other in amazement. You could have heard a pin drop in that room! They did not know how to react or what to say.

I was told that I answered everything they needed to know, and I received a great applause after I spoke. There were cheers and applause from Mr. and Mrs. Wagner, my mother Sandy Kellar, my best friend Lisa Davis, and special supporter Earl Wall.

Returning to my seat in the back of the room, Don Neilson, the Sykes Administrative Review Committee Chairman, thanked me. Then, Julie Risher, police attorney, and Angela Carmen, city attorney, took me outside to talk. Others followed, including Mark Rabil, Phoebe Zerwick, Jennifer Thompson, Lyn Warmoth-Boyd, Dan Galendo, Lieutenant Ferrelli, and Chief Norris. Everyone appeared to be stunned by the information and case details I provided. Chief Norris quickly apologized for not personally following up with me.

I began saving information in December 2003 because I now had positive proof that there was a connection between our cases. Richard had called me for two years trying to get to know me, trying to get a comfort level with me so I would open up and talk with them. On Martin Luther King Day 2004, I told them, especially Mark, that I would not speak or do anything that would cause problems, or jeopardize Darryl's people and the police from working together.

I did not want people pointing fingers at me and saying I interfered with the city's work, or that I was responsible for the delay in releasing Darryl Hunt. I did not go to his exoneration hearing because I knew that my identity would be revealed. My parents were also very concerned about me going to the hearing. My thoughts and prayers were there.

Phoebe called many times wanting to help me tell my story. She is a very good investigative reporter. My mother-in-law went to her grave angry with me because I would not talk. I met Phoebe at the hospital when my mother-in-law was taken there by ambulance in May 2004. One of her final wishes was to see me meet Phoebe, which I did on May 3rd, five days before she died on Mother's Day. It sounded so final when Phoebe said goodbye to my mother-in-law. She brought a framed copy of the December 19, 2003 article and told Mary that she had made a difference in the life of Darryl Hunt, and in the Winston-Salem community. Mary Lane did what the police refused to do. She did what they should have done. She did what several of us had tried to do years ago.

My last meeting with Crump we were standing in the lobby of the police department, and he was seeing me out. I will never forget looking up at him and saying, "Wouldn't it be wild if one day we found out that Deborah's attacker and my attacker was the same person."

Detective Crump actually told me that I needed to get on with my life. He told me that I was fortunate to be alive, and that I lived but Deborah died.

Crump said I could still have a life with my husband, can have children, and a future. Deborah could not do that. Remembering that today, I wonder if he was sincerely trying to help me, if I should feel guilty, or if this was a tactic to discourage me from pressing charges against Willard Brown by making me feel guilty.

His comments let me know that the police department's priority was the Sykes case, and that her case was more important than mine was. She had died. It was very important. Yet, there were many times that I felt neglected and forgotten.

Then, I would tell myself that I should be ashamed of myself for thinking that way. However, it was true. I felt like I had been put on a shelf, and I felt as if they were so focused on Deborah that the police could not think about me or dedicate appropriate resources to solve my case.

If they had thought about me, we could have gotten through this a long time ago. The fact that I lived and Deborah died does not negate or lessen what happened to me. It is not a trade off, one for the other.

It was stressful for everybody. I think about Jim Daulton, who was a detective for the Sykes crime, and eventually demoted along with others who were reprimanded. His peers thought he did not have enough experience to work this crime. He had only worked with juveniles cases prior to being assigned to the Sykes murder case.

This entire process has been a circus. There were so many things done to discourage me from prosecuting Willard Brown. I know today when Jim Daulton passed away that he too was a Christian, doing the best with what he had to work with.

I asked Lieutenant Ferrelli if I could review my crime scene pictures, and he said he thought I could. When I received the answer, "Yes," I asked if Mark Rabil could come with me. Lieutenant Ferrelli and Chief Norris discussed the request, and wanted to know why I would want Mark Rabil present when I viewed the photographs.

My heart told me many times that Mark was trying to do the right thing.

Chief Norris called me five times one Wednesday evening, trying to explain why she wanted just me. She said the committee wants to be the one to make full disclosure. I told her I understood, even though I was disappointed. The next night was a committee meeting and Chief Norris came in and sat down behind me. She told me she had been thinking about my request, and that Mark Rabil could accompany me to look at the pictures.

I was very relieved that I did not have to do this alone. Mark Rabil was actually shocked that he would be allowed to be there. We both went to the police station to review my crime scene pictures. Mark said he did not know how I managed to change Chief Norris' mind, and I replied, "I just asked sweetly."

I have fully cooperated with the police department and I have not requested much from them. I was glad the police changed their mind, and I did not have to go by myself. I was doing this more for Mark's sake so he could understand the full picture. We wanted to look at the evidence that I was told had been destroyed, which it had been.

I wanted Mark to know what happened to me, how it happened, and all the details of the crime. The current police investigators said they did not know where the pictures came from that were on their computers.

Some of the pictures were missing. I do not know if someone hid the pictures. Many times I felt that the police manipulated us like puppets. Otherwise they would have admitted they made mistakes, and apologized. That is really what I have expected for everyone. I expected an apology. Lee Garrity did apologize during the release and review of the four cases. Mr. Garrity told me he was sorry for the way I was treated. I thanked him and told him, that it meant a lot to me for him to say that.

Detective Miller says he does not remember my case. I wonder why? Is my value as a human being so slight that Detective Miller lost all memory of me and my case? Was this his opinion when he was the lead detective on my case from February 2, 1985 through May 1985, and his responsibility was to find the man who raped and tried to kill me? He provided the picture of Willard Brown to Detective Crump in May 1985. You have a mother that has lost her daughter that she loved very, very much; you have an innocent man sitting in prison, all of his attorney's, Mr.

Ferguson, Mark Rabil, Ben Dowling-Sendor, and others trying to obtain his release. And, then, there is me.

I realize that many people have mixed emotions about the Darryl Hunt case, and some people believe he was involved in the Sykes case. They believe that, although he did not rape her, he was there at the time of her attack, and assisted in her murder. That comes from public comments.

Brown was there, but not Darryl. Who were the other men on the street that morning with Deborah? People need second chances to do what is right. As hard as it is, people need to forgive one another!

People just cannot understand how an innocent man could be convicted twice if he were not guilty. *The Trials of Darryl Hunt* documentary helps to explain this. It was not Darryl's DNA that matched the crime; it was Willard Brown's DNA. From my own experience, I know the violent nature of Brown, and that is all I need to know.

The screening at the Stevens Center, *The Trials of Darryl Hunt* answered a lot for me. It was very kind of Mark Rabil, Jennifer Thompson, Darryl Hunt, and the Commission to give my husband and me tickets so we could see the whole story. It was interesting to sit in an audience that did not know I was there. I heard their emotions, gasps, and cheers.

I admire Hunt for not accepting a lesser charge that could have secured his release from prison years earlier. He maintained his innocence all along. If you are truly innocent, you will not accept blame and responsibility for the crime.

I admire Darryl's spirit of forgiveness. That is something we both have in common—a forgiving spirit. Willard Brown will probably never confess to his crime against me. Lieutenant Ferrelli said that he did not think he would confess because I beat him at his own game. I punked Willard Brown; I took his gun; I took his knife; I escaped. I fought him as a man would fight, and I won. Brown will never confess to his actions against me, if for no other reason than ego, and he was probably still drunk or stoned. It would make him look weak in prison.

I was fortunate to have driven further away from downtown Winston-Salem the morning of February 2, 1985. Those extra minutes provided me the opportunity to think about my situation, pray to God for his intervention, and plan how I was going to handle what I knew was coming. It also put me in a place where there were houses nearby and I could run to escape from Willard Brown. My husband Scott says that emotions and adrenaline flowed through me that day like those of a prizefighter who was going for the knockout punch.

If Brown had not insisted on driving away from the downtown area, it is highly possible that I would not be alive today. There would have been no reactionary time, or time to think. The attack would have happened right then, right there, and there might not have been anywhere to run to for shelter.

I also realized that I was truly protected and blessed because Willard Brown did not keep my drivers license or any type of identification. If he had, he would have had my name, address, and other information about me that could have been used to find me again.

Tracy Combs, reporter for the Winston-Salem Journal, wanted to do a published interview with me, but I said "No." She would have had to use my name in her story, which would have exposed me at a time when I would have been in grave danger. I was protected even then.

No, Willard Brown will never admit what he did to me. It is more than admitting guilt to multiple capital criminal offenses; in Brown's mind, it is shameful to him to realize that a woman got the best of him. His mind must be full of rage at the very thought of my escaping from him.

It is a great feeling to know that I succeeded in this situation. It is only by the grace of God! Brown will never tell the truth about what happened. He refused to swear on the Bible in court. As I watched Brown in court being convicted of his crime against Deborah Sykes, I really thought he might be mentally handicapped. When the judge asked him questions, Brown appeared incapable of speech, shaking his head 'No' or 'Yes'. When his answer would be yes, he would shake his head no, or visa versa. I now realize that was an act to gain pity. That was the mentality he was trying to portray.

I sat in the courtroom, and heard Pete Clary, his defense attorney, talk about Willard Brown's life. He had a pitiful childhood, only two friends, and was arrested when he was ten-years-old. Later, I saw the interviews with Cameron Kent and Mary Ann Sheboy, and Brown answered questions and had no problem speaking.

I do not feel sorry for him; he did what he did. But, like I said before, I do forgive him. I have prayed for him many times. I have prayed for God to remove my enemies and allow me peace of mind and heart.

When I made my statement to the committee, I did everything possible to tell them how grateful I am to God for what He has done for me. I told the committee that I had gone on with my life. I went forward thinking that the police department had exhausted every resource that they could have used to try to solve my crime. Unfortunately, that was not the case, which I later found out.

It was very important to me that I have the opportunity to meet the man that saved my life. I understood that this man was not at home when the detectives returned to question him.

Willard Brown was standing at the edge of the woods, but Miller told me that Wagner did not see him.

Maybe Detective Miller took the word of the officer on the scene. I still cannot understand why the detectives would not go back to the source, Mr. Wagner. He was step one, an eyewitness.

Detective Miller had the footprints, and pictures of them. In fact, that was the only picture that Miller would ever show me of the crime investigation over the last 22 years.

I was only permitted to see one picture with Detectives Miller and Barker in 1985. Detective Miller said the pictures were too traumatic for me to view. My account of what happened was told through those pictures, as I have viewed them today.

I believe Eric Saunders, Assistant District Attorney, tried

to keep me quiet. I felt he bottled me up, and I remember thinking how unfair it was. Nobody ever allowed me to speak publicly about my case without being identified. I did not want my entire family exposed to the media frenzy, nor did I want reporters camped on my doorstep.

I still need to know exactly what impact my case had on Brown's sentencing. I believe the details and aspects of my case were used as a bargaining tool in the sentencing of Willard Brown for the Sykes murder.

I want to see the discovery evidence. I told Eric Saunders that I wanted my name used in the discovery evidence so that there would be no question about Brown's involvement.

I need to know the truth of why my case was put on the back burner and never taken seriously. I need to know why I was given false information, and discouraged from prosecuting Brown. I need to understand why the police department refused to compare the evidence between these crimes and find the true criminal.

I testified before the Sykes Review Committee exactly 21 years after I was attacked, on February 2, 2006. This is extremely significant to me. I am coming full circle in my life. As I was called forward to speak, I noticed an opening in the tables just wide enough for me to stand. I wanted to be close to the people on this committee; I wanted to fill the empty spot like a piece of the puzzle.

This is my testimony to the Sykes Review Committee on 2/2/06.

My name is Regina and 21 years ago tomorrow, I was labeled by the Winston-Salem Journal as The Integon Victim. My life was forever changed on February 2, 1985. There were many things going right then. I had fallen in love, become engaged, and received a promotion at work, which fortunately, required overtime. This is the reason I was downtown on a Saturday morning.

I have come here today at the request of Lieutenant Joseph Ferrelli and the Sykes Review Committee. It was requested that I be interviewed and allow an audio video recording to be made, summarized in written form and this would be presented to the Committee. I have allowed the Winston-Salem Police Department and others to represent me for 21 years, and the police assured me early on that they had done what they could. It is time for me to speak. I have come here to make a public statement in regard to the way my case was handled up to this point.

On the day of the attack after I was released from the hospital, I went to the police department, filed a police report, and looked at hundreds of pictures until 8:00 that night. I was 19-years-old and had never seen, heard, or experienced anything so cruel and controlling. I was terrified.

On Day Two while riding with the detectives, I told Detectives Bill Miller and Mike Barker that a Winston-Salem Journalist had visited my Mom and Dad's home that morning. I was considering doing an interview with her, however, when she got to the house, I declined because she said she would have to use my name. The practice of releasing names at the Journal has since changed. Detective Miller told me that it was a good thing that I did not talk with her because "she was gay." I was shocked. I didn't care about her sexual preferences, if that was even true, I just wanted to find out who the man was that tried to cut my head off and tried to kill me.

Before I came to the Police Department on 2/7/85 when I was doing a composite sketch with an artist, my future mother-in-law insisted that I ask the detectives about the Deborah Sykes murder. I specifically asked Detective Mike Barker (Detective Bill Miller was away from where we were) if Mike thought the same person that got me was the same one that got Deborah Sykes? Has the information been compared? Mike did not know and deferred the question Detective Miller when he returned. Detective Miller walked away again and when he returned, he said in a very firm voice his answer. "They already had the men or man that raped and killed Deborah Sykes in jail." Detective Miller told me that "they didn't want to do anything that would make people ask questions or put doubts in people's minds because it could hurt the case against the people in jail."

They assured me that Darryl Hunt and Sammy Mitchell were big men and both six feet tall. My attacker was approximately 5'6." I also asked if there were any other victims that had gone through what I had and Detective Miller said not that he knew of. Detective Miller said there might be other detectives working on cases. My hope was something like the movies and most of the time the cops get the bad guys.

When I returned to the crime scene I explained to Detective Miller what happened, where it happened and how it happened. I could tell his mind was really thinking about everything I had said. He told me the next week that they were hoping to do a segment on Crime Stopper's. They were hoping a re-enactment would help solve the crime. Detective Miller said something to me that day that really upset me. He said, "We had to make sure that you didn't do this to yourself." Was it that he did not believe me? Here I stood with 30 stitches in my head and face, not counting the cuts to my neck and hands. I had been taken at gunpoint, pistol-whipped in the head, down the left eye and more. He knew I was really upset. Later he apologized and said I would be amazed at how many people accuse others of committing crimes. He later told me that he was sorry.

I returned to work two weeks after my attack. The week before, Detective Miller, my fiancé, and I went back into the Integon building to meet with the Head of Security. I was seeking a comfort level to return to work. I stood in the hallway alone with Detective Miller right before we left, and told him that I had been thinking about something. He listened as I told him that I thought the charges of attempted murder should be added.

I told him once again when my attacker had pulled out the knife and reached from behind me, he had every intention to slit my throat or cut my head off. The only reason he did not was because I tucked my head down and my chin took the cut. Detective Miller's response about adding the charges was "We'll see." It was my understanding that there were not any fingerprints left by Willard Brown as he wore gloves that day, not fingerless as my mother-in-law had dreamed on the night after the attack. All of the blood found matched mine. I do not know what comparisons were made to Deborah Sykes.

Later, I began working with Detective Carter Crump. He notified me that an arrest had been made and he wanted to do a lineup at the sheriff's department. During the lineup, I expected the lineup of men to be behind the big glass window that you always see in the movies. I was taken up on a steel elevator that had a small window in the door. I was again terrified. I was psyching myself up to go up to the men and stand face to face.

I had determined in my mind that I was going to have them say the things that were said to me during the attack. Right before they got ready to start letting me view the people, they said I could not speak to them. The people with me said they would ask the questions. This blew my confidence. When I put my face up to the window, I saw Willard Brown standing to the left of where the door would have opened. I gasped and backed up from the window, feeling the fear run throughout my body. My knees became weak and I thought I was going to throw-up. I was 80-85% sure that it was Brown. I was afraid of accusing and putting an innocent man behind bars.

I have worked very hard cooperating with the police since Day One. I walked downtown, rode with the police downtown, and rode the bus one Saturday morning to try and find my attacker. After identifying Willard Brown, I asked Detective Crump "Just bring me a person or one piece of evidence so we can go forward." That was in 1986. I even asked him to go back and check the records on Brown to see if he was in prison during the attacks.

The State Correctional Center gave out information that Brown was in prison when Deborah was attacked. Brown did not have a history of this kind of behavior according to police records. Detective Crump said that he would not take this to the District Attorney until I decided whether or not to press charges. At that time, I did not even know what a DA was. I do not know what Detective Crump's final actions were. Without more evidence, I did not press charges.

Detective Crump was very supportive during this time; all of the detectives were. I told Detective Crump that I understood how the height of an attacker could be different from what people saw.

My case was inactive and closed many times. The Committee specifically asked if my case closed in May of 1986 and the answer is yes. The evidence was destroyed 3 years after the attack in 1989. When the evidence was offered to me, I did not want my clothes back or my coat. I did not want the knife that nearly took my life. I did ask Detective Crump at some point if the Police Department would do a voice recognition. Detective Crump left the room and returned after asking someone the question. It seems like it was a female. He asked me if I would press charges if the voice recognition was a match, and I told him I could not answer that. I told him that my attacker had a deep gruff voice. He agreed that Brown's voice sounded like that. He said if I could not say if I would press charges that he was told that it could not be done. He was told that there was not enough manpower. What happened to the paper that I wrote down the words said to me by my attacker?

I think Brown was in prison at that time. I had already asked early on about comparing the shoe size to Brown's foot size. I later found out that the shoeprints left in the mud that day were from Converse tennis shoes. I asked Detective Miller and Barker to send someone out to the drink houses that Willard Brown was known to hang out in. They were unable to do that.

There was and has been a tremendous amount of time devoted to gathering information regarding the Sykes investigation and the re-investigation. Each time I was asked questions. Deborah's family deserves to know what happened!!! I had heard so much about Deborah Sykes case that I told my Mother that I was upset because I felt neglected. At one point, when I asked him about my case, Detective Crump said with encouragement, "I should be thankful that I didn't turn out like Deborah Sykes."

I AM very grateful to God for hearing my silent prayer and saving my life that day. Detective Crump said, "I have *my life and my husband and can have kids and go to with my life and Deborah can't do that." That is what I did. I brushed myself off and with God watching over me, with the help of the loving family and friends around me, I went forward with my life never thinking I would face this again. I thought that the Police Department had exhausted its resources regarding my case. Unfortunately, that was not the case as I later found out.*

Prior to January 7, 2004, I talked to Phoebe Zerwick with the Winston-Salem Journal. I declined to be interviewed many, many times. I allowed the city police to do what they needed to do. I told her one of the things I hoped to do was meet the man who saved my life. I understood from Detective Miller and Barker that this man was not at home the next day when the detectives returned to the crime scene. Within the next week, Detective Miller told me that he had contacted Mr. Wagner and thanked him for me and Mr. Wagner said that he did not see my attacker. There was a comment in my report that a statement was made by a woman confirming that she saw and heard my VW.

On 1/23/2006, I called Mr. Wagner during my lunch hour. He told me that after 2/2/85, no one ever mentioned the attack or came back to ask questions. Then he remembered Phoebe coming back a couple of years ago following up on what I had told her. She told Mr. Wagner she was going to write a story. Mr. Wagner said he never saw anything in the paper. When he told me the police had never returned to question him, I just broke down and cried. I asked Mr. Wagner if he would come with me tonight to confirm my statement. With your permission, please allow me to introduce the man who saved my life, David Wagner.

One thing I do not understand is how I asked Detective Miller for a police report after the attack and another time after that only to receive a copy of my hospital report. It has not really been a thought until all these questions have come up. I was permitted to review a copy of my report at the Police Department last year with Detective Mike Rowe.

The detectives earlier and Detective Rowe walked by my

side like one of my brothers. My police report has not been noted as well as it could have been documented with details of research and findings from 1985-1990's. After the attack, I told my story to Detective Miller who wrote it down. My parents were with me during this time. When Detective Miller gave it back to me, he asked me to read and confirm the report. I told him that there were things that were different. I told him that I did not take the belt off Willard Brown (even with a gun pointed 3 inches from my face) that I played dumb and said I did not know how. It was like an Army belt. I told him that after Brown raped me on the back seat of the car, he made me get outside on the right side of the car and intended to continue his attack from behind me. Brown was not successful. I moved three more times and then Brown told me if I didn't hold still that he was going to put himself (penis) somewhere else that I didn't want. At the time I told Detective Miller my story I had left these details out, remembering as a flashback while confirming my report, however, that was never noted in my report. I specifically asked Detective Miller to note that I did not do as I was ordered. Detective Miller did NOT note this. I want to emphasize that my report was not properly documented.

The Winston-Salem Journal does its best to tell the news! I see that a lot of effort goes into calls, interviews, and the information that is reported. I quit watching the news for a long time and did not even read the paper. Like the opinion of the radio station JOY FM, 91.3 FM, it disappoints me that there is so much good in the world that could be talked about and yet we hear so many negative things. I feel that the Journal put a lot of pressure on people about stories.

I saw this when my mother-in-law was being interviewed for her January 2004 story. I think that others thought that I was releasing information about my case; however, I was not. The whole story does need to be told. My mother-in-law called Phoebe in the latter part of 2003 at the Winston-Salem Journal and was then put in touch with Mark Rabil. I told Detective Mike Rowe and Darryl Hunt's defense attorney Mark Rabil in 2004 and 2005 that I would be willing to talk with them, the police department and Tom Keith together but it was never permitted.

My mother-in-law instigated Mark Rabil's inquiries. I guess the police assumed that I knew. They said they re-opened the case and planned to bring 404B charges against Willard Brown. My mother-in-law was diagnosed with cancer and died in May 2004. I learned about my mother-in-law approaching Phoebe and Mark Rabil by her telling me at Christmas 2003 and by reading the minutes of the Sykes Review Committee. The Police Department told me that they solved the crime with DNA evidence, which is true.

The only person I have ever met in the District Attorney's office was Eric Saunders in 1/2004. I met Tom Keith after Willard Brown was sentenced to prison for 21 years and 3 months. I never met Don Tisdale or Warren Sparrow. I remember receiving two phone calls from an attorney's office. This was before and after I was married in May 1985. The one question I remember is if Darryl and/or Sammy were the person that attacked me? I told them no and that I had seen pictures in the police department. They were not my attacker. I do not remember whether I was told about the January 1985 attack years ago. I did not know of any other similar attacks except Deborah. After 2001, I remember being contacted at my current job by Charles "Slick" Poteat, who asked if I worked at Integon then. I declined to talk with him that day. I am glad I have had the opportunity to talk with him today.

As the time drew closer to Brown's trial, I was given frequent status updates by Detective Mike Rowe. On November 19, 2004, Detective Rowe called and told me to mark my calendar for December 13-20th. On December 6, 2004, Detective Rowe called to explain what the DA was proposing for Willard Brown, which was 21 years and three months. Originally, Brown would be in prison until he was 70 years old. I had confirmed to Mike Rowe on 7/8/2004 that I would not press charges because Brown would be in prison until he was age 70.

In December 2004, Mike said that Eric Saunders said

that I am part of the plea. I am the reason he took a plea so he would not have to face the other charges. Detective Rowe confirmed that Eric Saunders and Tom Keith never told him about the 12/4/2004 newspaper article and the final charges against Brown. I asked Detective Rowe, "What are your intentions?" Detective Rowe said since there is no trial, I am not part of this. Other charges will not be brought up. Brown denied charges against me. I remind myself that he also denied any charges against Deborah Sykes. Detective Mike Rowe explained that the media release "Similar Case" was a factor in Brown taking the plea. Press releases were other factors.

In 2005, I called Eric Saunders to ask for my police report and his response was that I need closure. He said it does not help viewing this information again. He said that I needed professional help. If I have it in a place that I can look at it over and over again, then it won't be closure. I felt like I was the hot potato being passed. Mike can't release, Eric won't release. I even called the courthouse to learn that they do not have a copy of my police report.

Yet today, everyone still wants me to answer questions like it was yesterday. On 12/23/2004 at 9:30 a.m. I called Vivian Burke regarding my police report. At 10:30, Chief Norris called and talked to me. When Chief Norris visited my home on 12/28/2004, she said it was a new policy that Police reports would not be released if a case has not been prosecuted. Chief Norris said that I am driving the boat. I have to decide whether to prosecute or not. She assured me that the police department would not do anything to hurt or harm me. We talked more about the improvements in the current Criminal Division and the attack. I told Chief Norris about the questions I asked Detectives Bill Miller, Carter Crump and the responses. Chief Norris took notes and was going to find out the following:

1. Would Brown automatically be released in 21 years and 3 months?

2. Was Detective Mike Rowe able to give me all of my report?

3. Why was I told that Brown was in prison during the

Deborah Sykes murder, but yet he was out in June?

4.Chief Norris was going to ask Tom Keith about pressing charges. Was my case used as a plea bargain? Chief Norris understood that it was all Sykes related.

5.Chief Norris was going to find out if there is an internal investigation in the Police Department. I noted 1/28/2005 and still today, I have not received a response from Chief Norris, only from Detective Rowe calling on her behalf.

Then, to find out that my police report was given to Phoebe on 2/3/2005? What a shocker! I was told that this was a misunderstanding of this being released.

On 3/24/2005, my sister-in-law met me for lunch and asked me if I had seen the letter dated 1/25/2005 from Tom Keith to Mayor Allen Joines that appeared in the Winston-Salem Journal. Help me out here. I am just a little confused.

When I met the Sykes family during the Brown trial in December 2004, they were a blessing to me, it gave me great comfort to know that Deborah Sykes had asked the Lord Jesus Christ to be her personal Savior. I come here now to be part of the solution, not the problem. I will be praying that God will give you wisdom to find out the whole truth for all of us. Please let us know what went wrong!

CHAPTER NINE

Why God May Allow
Certain Problems

1 Peter 3: 12-13
For the eyes of the Lord are on the righteous and his ears are attentive to their prayer. But the face of the Lord is against those who do evil. Even if you should suffer...you are blessed. Do not fear; do not be frightened. But in your hearts, set apart Christ as Lord.

1 Peter 2:19-20
For it is commendable if a man bears up under the pain of unjust suffering...If you suffer for doing good and you endure it, this is commendable before God. Christ suffered for you, leaving you an example.

2 Corinthians 12:9
My grace is sufficient for you, for my power is made perfect in weakness.

John 16:13
But when the Friend comes, the Spirit of Trust, he will take you by the hand and guide you into all the truth there is.

I could say, why me? I have had mishaps, from a pony kicking me in the mouth and neck, a broken arm, suffering from health issues, and much more.

Why did this happen to me? I was not a bad person. I

never hurt anyone, and tried to live a good life; yet, I was so viciously attacked. Why would God allow this horrible thing to happen to me, and allow Brown to escape punishment and accountability for what he did?

It is not just about me. I am sure that there are people everyday who ask themselves these same questions. People do not understand why they experience pain or suffering.

People probably do not understand why good things happen to bad people. Moreover, they do not understand why wicked people seem to get all the breaks.

No one is protected from suffering or adversity. Many suffer because of sickness, or loss of a loved one. Others suffer because they are victims of circumstances over which they have no control. Some people bring suffering on themselves through the bad decisions they make, or by abusing their own bodies. Wrong choices eventually come back to haunt you.

Still others, like me, suffer because of something that was done to us.

God may permit suffering in our lives so we can learn to respond to problems the right way. We can learn about God's direction for our lives as we are inspected, corrected and protected. If we submit ourselves to God's will in our lives, we will be perfected.

Jesus suffered greatly in order to leave us a beautiful example of His love and mercy.

Sometimes God permits us to suffer to teach us that pain is a part of life. Nowhere in the Bible does it say that we will not suffer. God may also allow suffering because of our own sin and disobedience.

The real solution to dealing with the "Why Me" is to understand that God did not promise us a perfect life that is free of trouble. He promised that He would be with us *in time of trouble*. Therein lies the difference.

Some of the most pathetic people in the world are those who, in the midst of their problem or suffering, wallow in self-pity and bitterness and blame God for their circumstances.

But God tells us that we will be blessed if, in the middle

of agony and despair, we look to our Heavenly Father and be thankful for his love and presence.

God may work in our lives through our suffering to inspire others. If we trust Him throughout it all, we could be setting a good example for another person. We could inspire others to deal with their own adversity.

These are character-building experiences in our lives. Sometimes we must look back and use those experiences to move forward, help ourselves, and help others that God puts in our future.

Of course, no one wants to build his or her character by enduring kidnapping, rape, and stabbing! That is not what I am saying. What I am saying is that God was with me throughout the entire attack. He never left me. I learned that He will be with me, protect me, and save me if I put myself in His hands. Naturally, there were times when I thought I could not go on any longer, but the Lord kept me moving forward. *Genesis 28:15 I am with you and will watch over you wherever you go, and I will bring you back...I will not leave you until I have done what I have promised you.*

Proverbs 12:21 clearly tells us that "there shall no evil happen to the just..." Why then do bad things happen to good people? There are a couple of things wrong with these questions.

First, there are no good people in the world. The Bible says that "all have sinned and come short of the glory of God (Romans 3:23), and "there is none that doeth good, no not one" (Romans 3:12). Therefore, all people are deserving of God's wrath and judgment.

The reason we wonder why bad things happen to us is that we think we are so good and so deserving. We do not fully understand that any good thing that God does for us is through His mercy, grace, and love.

Therefore, when something bad happens to us, our first reaction is usually, "Why me?" Or we may even get mad at God because we were expecting a different outcome.

Second, if a person is saved and loves God, everything that happens is for his good and God's glory. The problem with people is that they do not stop and consider the purpose and God's eventual plan. We do not see life from God's perspective. His ways are not our ways, and His thoughts are not our thoughts. What looks like evil and injustice from our perspective may actually be a way to bring blessing to not only us, but to many other people.

My purpose is to help others through my experience. By telling my story, I may be able to connect with victims who are struggling to find the answers and strength to live.

I want to provide comfort and hope that God is in control, and has a purpose and plan for our lives. Even in times of deepest despair, we can just whisper His name, and He is with us. There is tremendous assurance in the knowledge of His almighty presence in my life. While I was fighting for my life, God was there, giving me strength and determination to overcome.

Do not get the impression that bad things only happen to good people. Bad things also happen to bad people. The difference is that a Child of God has the supernatural, indwelling presence of God to help them deal with the situation. By determining to listen to the Holy Spirit within us, God can help us make the right decisions. He is always there to warn us if we are making a mistake, or doing something that could hurt us. The Holy Spirit speaks through inner feelings, not through the head, but through the heart. The more time I spend with God, the better I am able to discern His voice guiding and directing me. How hopeless it must be to be without God!

We also do not need to spend one moment worrying about why the bad person "gets away with it." That person is not really getting away with anything. God knows everything. He knows the intent of our hearts, our actions, our thoughts, and feelings.

We can take comfort in believing that there will come a day when God will provide complete justice for every evil act. A person might commit an atrocious crime, and never spend one day in prison. But God will judge. His word tells us that everyone will reap what they sow.

The reality is *life is not always fair*. People commit crimes, and sometimes, are not punished quickly or even at all. That is what we see in our judicial system today. Someone may commit a murder, be arrested, go to jail, get out on bail, and be back on the street again in a few days time.

Sometimes criminals go unpunished. Sometimes innocent people are unjustly punished. That is true of every country on the face of the earth. Evil exists in a corrupt world. Because we live in this world, it affects all of us in very real ways.

The most common tendency when we are mistreated is to seek revenge. I will always choose to give it to God and watch how he may choose to bless it. I believe that "spite" works does fall on the "spiter." Everyone has been mistreated at some point in her or his life. However, the way we deal with it will determine how quickly our hearts and minds heal, and how quickly we can overcome the suffering.

Wherever you are right now, you can look around and see people who have some stories in their lives. Some are happy; many are sad.

God has given me the gift of being able to think before I speak with discernment and thoughtfulness. It takes a lot to make me angry, and even then, God brings me back to prayerfulness so he can take my concern and work it out according to his purpose.

I am the oldest girl and middle child. I learned early on that I do not always get my way and I cannot always be first. I am glad God gave the example in life of turning the other cheek. Again, I am grateful to my parents for the way they have raised five children.

By allowing God to be alive and at work in our lives, we can overcome the temptation to "get even." I believe mean things we do can come back to haunt you. We can focus on forgiveness and let God handle the rest. How marvelous to know that He is in control. I do not have to spend one moment thinking about how to deal with it. God will deal with it for me. I will give it to Him and not take it back!

He has proven His promises to me repeatedly throughout my life. My situation, the events with Willard Brown, and the treatment I received from the detectives and investigators, everything I have endured and suffered, will all be put to right in God's time and in His way.

Of course, that does not mean that we stop looking for answers, and stop trying to make process improvements to prevent mistakes from happening again. That is one of the primary reasons I agreed to speak to the Sykes Administrative Review Committee in February 2006. Even in June 2006, the committee was hoping to conclude their research by August or September. It was actually February 19, 2007 before the Committee published their findings and recommendations. Thank you Lieutenant Ferrelli for personally delivering my copy to my home at 10 o'clock that night.

The fact is, bad things *do* happen; no one is exempt.God gave me the most incredible testimony of His mercy, saving grace, and love. When I tell my story, I can see God working in the hearts of grown men and women, who are brought to tears upon hearing about my ordeal.

God allowed me to experience the most incredible testimony of His mercy, saving grace, and love that can bring grown men and women to tears when they hear the story.

If we put our faith and trust in God, we can rest assured that there will be a purpose in our suffering and justice at the end of the road.

Remember, look for how God will bless a situation. God made His own son suffer the cross for me. He certainly will not forsake me now.

I encourage you to take time to read the 106-page report with 9000 pages of appendices covering the 1980's to current date.

CHAPTER TEN

I Have Come By
The Way of The Cross

Romans 8:31-39

If God be for us, who can be against us? He that spared not his own Son, but delivered him up for us all, how shall he not with him also freely give us all things? Who shall lay anything to the charge of God's elect?

It is God that justifieth. Who is he that condemneth? It is Christ that died, yea rather, that is risen again, who is even at the right hand of God, who also maketh intercession for us. Who shall separate us from the love of Christ?

Shall tribulation, or distress, or persecution, or famine, or nakedness, or peril, or sword? As it is written, For thy sake we are killed all the day long; we are accounted as sheep for the slaughter. Nay, in all these things we are more than conquerors through him that loved us.

For I am persuaded, that neither death, nor life, nor angels, nor principalities, nor powers, nor things present, nor things to come, nor height, nor depth, nor any other creature, shall be able to separate us from the love of God, which is in Christ Jesus our Lord.

Lamentations 3:25

The Lord is good unto them that wait for him, to the soul that seeketh him.

Throughout this book, I have talked about the saving mercy and grace of God's love. This book would not be complete if it did not include the details of how you can experience the awesome power of God in your own life. Sometimes, what Satan meant for evil, God means for good.

I want you to see the tremendous plan of salvation as God states in His Word. God's plan is the one whereby we can be saved. It is the one plan that gives us assurance of our salvation, and whereby we can know with certainty that we are going to heaven when we leave this world.

You will never experience true joy and happiness without the Lord in your life. The plan of salvation is clear, simple, and plain. It is free, open, and available to everyone.

Romans 5:1 states, *"Being therefore justified by faith, we have peace with God through our Lord Jesus Christ."* We can have complete peace. It is a wonderful thing to be able to have peace in your heart, regardless of your situation.

When I was kidnapped, I called on the Lord Jesus Christ to help me. In the midst of that horrific attack, I had peace knowing that He was with me. I knew that, whatever the outcome, I was eternally saved. If I had died that day, my soul would have been immediately transported to the throne of God. There is no peace outside of Him.

The only way we can have peace with God is through our Lord Jesus Christ. There is no other way. Leave Him out, and you will have no peace with God; it must be through Him. Psa*lms 13:5-6 But I trust in your unfailing love; my heart rejoices in your salvation. I will sing to the Lord, for he has been good to me.*

The one thing that troubles people is the *sin* question. Jesus forever settled that question on Calvary when He died on the cross. He paid the ultimate price so that we could have forgiveness of sin through Him. He went to the cross for *you!* If there had been no other person in the whole world that was lost and needed salvation, He would still have suffered the cross for you!

Many people have their own personal opinion about the way to make it into heaven. Some people believe that if they do the best they can, try to stay out of trouble, and get along with their fellow man, God will accept them into heaven.

Others believe that it does not matter what they practice as long as they are sincere and genuine about it. Still others believe that everyone will go to heaven, even though they take different roads to get there.

There is only one way—through Jesus Christ. That fact is based on God's word, which is wholly reliable and trustworthy. It does not matter what we say about the true plan of salvation; what matters is what God says about getting to heaven. You may have your own beliefs, but they are worthless if they disagree with what God says.

God's plan of salvation is based on the following principles:

1. There is a heaven and a hell.

2. God desires that no one go to hell, but that everyone go to heaven

3. God made a plan so that anyone who wants to go to heaven can go

4. If we try to get there any other way outside of God's way, we will not make it, in spite of our sincerity or good intentions.

Romans 3:10 *"As it is written, there is none righteous, no, not one."* Everyone has sinned. We were born into a sinful world with a sin nature. Romans 3:23 *"For all have sinned, and come short of the glory of God."*

God sent his only son into the world as a sacrifice for sin. Jesus Christ willingly went to the cross for you and for me. He died, and rose again to prepare a way of salvation. His blood will cover our sins when we believe in him.

John 3:16 *"For God so loved the world that he gave his only begotten son that whosoever believeth in him should not perish but have everlasting life."*

The only way a person can be saved is by first confessing his sins. Luke 13:3 says, *"Except you repent, you shall likewise perish."* As we confess our sins to the Lord, and place our faith in his saving power and grace, and his finished work on the cross, He promises to forgive our sins.

Romans 3:24-26 *"Being justified freely by his grace*

through the redemption that is in Christ Jesus. Whom God hath set forth to be a propitiation through faith in his blood, to declare his righteousness for the remission of sins that are past, through the forbearance of God. To declare his righteousness, that he might be just, and the justifier of him that believeth in Jesus."

Examine your heart. Have you asked Jesus to forgive your sins, and save you? Salvation is a free gift! Place your faith in Jesus Christ. Ask him to forgive your sins, and come into your heart. He will save you, and prepare a home in Heaven for you.

Recite this simple prayer:

Dear Jesus,

I know that I have sinned and confess these sins right now. I pray to you to forgive me of my sins, cleanse my heart and soul, and save me through your saving blood. I receive you right now. Please come into my heart Lord Jesus.

Thank you God for allowing your son Jesus Christ to die on the cross for my sins. Lord, I pray that you would help me to know your love and will in my life. Help me to share what I have learned with others so we can all come to heaven where you are, preparing a place for those who believe in you.

In Jesus precious name I pray,
Amen.

Epilogue

On February 19, 2007, The Sykes Administrative Review Committee released their long-awaited and anticipated official report on the Deborah Sykes homicide, the three other rape cases, and the 1983 Arthur Wilson homicide case. This report is 106 pages, with 38 appendix totaling almost 9000 pages. It carefully and comprehensively documents all that the city learned of the truth in these cases.

Darryl Hunt settled with the City of Winston-Salem for $1.65 million dollars in compensation for being falsely accused, convicted, and incarcerated.

The Sykes Administrative Report also fully corroborates my story. The report validates the details related to my case, and the fact that detectives did not use all available investigative methods to help me prove my case against Willard Brown.

Of special interest is the Committee's conclusion that the Police Department should have used Voice Recognition as part of the identification process in my situation. I requested Voice Recognition after I identified Willard Brown in the live line-up; however, I was told that it could not be done.

In addition, the Report verifies that the same detectives were working on my case at the same time they were working on the Deborah Sykes case. They knew about both cases; they either deliberately or negligently, did not compare the cases.

Keeping in mind that I was told "they did not want to do anything to put doubt in people's mind about the Hunt case," it is a logical assumption that my identification of Willard Brown, and the similar aspects of both cases, would have cast doubt on Hunt's guilt.

The Report, released by order of Superior Court Judge William Z. Wood, includes these findings:

Point # 3: The police either failed to see or document any connections that were made between the Deborah Sykes and Regina K. cases even when both were under investigation at the same time by the same detective.

Point # 4: The police either failed to consider, or to document after consideration, any investigative leads or evidence derived from the Linda E. and Kathleen D. cases, even after the same investigator worked on those cases, and the Sykes and my case.

Point # 14: Case files in these investigations were not always completed in a timely manner.

And, Point # 15: The police "marginalized Regina K. by not conducting a voice exemplar to include Brown, discouraging her from pressing charges, and failed to make an apparent connection to the Sykes case."

The city obtained court approval to release confidential personnel information. This included the Disciplinary Actions taken against Detective Daulton.

The official transcript of the disciplinary action taken against Daulton documents specific questions and answers regarding the District Attorney's strategy in prosecuting Darryl Hunt for the murder of Deborah Sykes, and their strategy in investigating other similar criminal cases.

The documented District Attorney's strategy adds further validity to my belief that the police department, detectives, investigators, and all people involved with my case, were deliberately keeping anything detrimental to the Hunt case out of court records. They did not want to damage their case against Hunt. Therefore, the strategy was to minimize, disregard, and neglect my case and me.

On page 11 of the transcript, it specifically states during testimony that the District Attorney's strategy was to keep anything detrimental to the prosecution's case against Hunt from coming out in court and to keep it away from the jury. Daulton affirmed this strategy under sworn testimony during the hearing.

Again, on page 14 of the transcript, Daulton confirmed that he was following instructions from the DA in not disclosing anything that might be detrimental to the State's case. Following this thought, it is further validation that Daulton's role in the investigation of my case would have been considered detrimental to the State's case against Darryl Hunt.

Therefore, no comparisons were made public. Also, on page 83 of the transcript, the DA again testifies that if there is evidence that is harmful to the case, he will not bring it out. By obvious conclusion, the DA and investigators would not openly associate my case with the Sykes case, and would withhold exculpatory evidence in order to successfully prosecute Hunt. My case in the media, therefore, was not exculpatory.

I refer to page 71 of the document, in which the District Attorney stated that he instructed his detectives and personnel to *"give the impression that you are the nicest guy around, and that you would help them if you could..."* Throughout the years, I had the impression that the police department was working with me, and I felt guilty when I doubted their sincerity. After reviewing this transcript, I now seriously doubt their intentions.

Perhaps those instructions to "give people the impression that you would help them" is standard procedure. I believe this is deceptive; they should have a sincere desire to help people. That should be the normal, everyday attitude of anyone working with the public.

Continuing through the official report, there is a section entitled "Closed Session Minutes." Contained within the minutes of March 9, 2006, is the detailed testimony of Daulton and Sergeant Byron. Sergeant Byron stated that Daulton told him to *"not put too much into his reports because information was being leaked to the Hunt defense team."*

It is a logical conclusion that the police department, detectives, investigators, and others associated with these cases made a deliberate and willful effort to create vague police reports, and avoid making the obvious comparisons between the Sykes case and the investigation into my case.

This same document also details the amazingly similar crime scene photographs of Deborah Sykes and me.

Detective Mike Rowe of the Winston-Salem Police Department filed a summary report in July, 2006, that details the investigative actions taken in my case. His report documents interviews with detectives assigned to my case in 1985—1989, and draws conclusions that are relevant to the claims made in my book. A few of those conclusions are:

•Part 2, page 62—Regina K File: My description of Willard Brown matches to the description of Deborah Sykes attacker. Captain Tesh stated the location of my attack and Sykes' attack was similar; the actions of the attacker were similar, and the photograph comparisons of Deborah and me looked alike.

•Page 68 confirms that Willard Brown was not in jail at the time of either of these crimes

•Captain Tesh asserts on page 71 that Willard Brown's photograph clearly shows the gap between his teeth. It is apparent that this validates my description of Brown during the original investigation. Again, in the initial SARC Report, Page 29, paragraph 2, Detective Rowe was able to compare Willard Brown's teeth and the slight gap between the front two teeth, and concluded that they were the same and matched the description that I had provided, discussed, and stated.

•Page 73 details an interview with Vicky Pearl, who stated that the Police Department had tunnel vision when comparing the Sykes murder and my case. She stated the similarities between the two crimes were apparent and that she brought this to the attention of the investigating officers. Pearl was told the same thing that I was told: *they had already arrested Hunt for the Sykes murder and did not want to create any doubt surrounding his guilt.*

•The report also documents the amazingly similar crime

scene photographs of Deborah Sykes and Me. Daulton's comment was that he only saw the Polaroid pictures Detective Miller made of me, and not the crime scene comparison photos. Yet, Daulton signed off on some of my reports.

On page 95, Section VII of the City Manager's Report, Lee Garrity states that I identified Williard Brown as my attacker from both photographic and in-person line-ups, and that I also insisted I could recognize my attacker's voice if I heard it again. The City Manager goes on to state that the way the Detectives treated me was "*simply unacceptable.*"

I think it is pathetic that Eric Saunders, who worked as the assistant DA, would not speak with the SARC committee and that Tom Keith, another DA, would not respond to me to answer the SARC questions. I called him several times and asked what charges would have been brought against Willard Brown, should the attempted murder charge been added, and what time would have been served by Willard Brown if he had been convicted of the charges against me. Would it have been more than 3-4 years, 5 years max?

Comparative data for similar situations include the Jennifer Thompson case versus Ronald Cotton. Cotton served 11 years for a crime against Thompson that he did not commit. There needs to be a law of accountability in Winston-Salem, if not the United States, that requires authorities to answer these types of questions in specific circumstances.

In the SARC Report, page 27, footnote 149, the report states that Brown was charged with first degree murder, first degree rape, first degree kidnapping, and robbery with a dangerous weapon in the Sykes case on December 22, 2003. However, on page 28, paragraph 2, the report states the Regina K. case involved kidnapping, rape and brutal assault. Why were the charges in my case so minimalized?

Why would I want to be represented by people who were unwilling to assist me? Upon meeting Eric Saunders, his first and more important question and comment to me was "*It was a good thing you didn't prosecute..*" I told him thank you, and that was what Mark Rabil said too. Mark

157

said it might have left Darryl Hunt in prison the rest of his life.

Later, when asking Saunders for my police report, he told me I needed closure, and that I did not need the report in a place I could look at it repeatedly. He said I needed professional help.

I find it very insulting that Eric Saunders would offer those condescending words to me, the victim. He has never been attacked himself, or been in my situation. His role as a paid public service professional should have been to offer support, and attempt to obtain some degree of justice for me through our legal system and process.

Tom Keith said, *"The justice system is broken,"* and stated that our prisons are built in poor rural counties in order to provide work for people. My question is, "How are we going to fix our justice system?"

I would like to recommend to future investigations that our modern technology of conference calling be used to include family members of the deceased victim, like Mrs. Jefferson, Deborah Sykes mother. She should have been allowed to listen to what was being said and documented.

I would also like to hear that microphones are used in our court systems so people in the audience do not have to strain to listen to every word being said by attorneys and court personnel.

On Page 6 of the SARC Report, the City Manager's Note said, "Detectives were not willing to send someone out to drink houses to ask questions." How far was the 1700 block of Claremont Avenue and 17th Street from 14th Street? That could have been where Brown became intoxicated before attacking us.

In the Report, page 7, paragraph 3, it states that Detectives Hicks and Miller drove Linda E. around town. When I asked the question, "Are there any similar cases?" Detective Miller's response was, *"No, not that I know of, but other detectives may be working on other cases."* That was a false and misleading statement. He was heavily involved in investigating Linda E.'s case already, and should have made the connection instantly. Instead, he lied to me.

From the text and documentation on page 8, section A, I would like to know if the composite drawing I made was the same as Hooper's drawing for either attackers. On page 32, item # 6, my question is, "Was my case ever discussed with the District Attorney's office?"

Again, on page 32, item #8, I would like to know what the upward channel of authority over Detectives Miller and Crump existed at that time. This would also apply to Raker, Cornantzer and Furman Mason.

Still on page 32, item #9, I have multiple questions. Were Willard Brown and Thomas acquainted? Were they in prison together and did they violate another prisoner's rights? Did Thomas live in High Point or Thomasville with Brown at any time?

On page 34, item # 11, it indicates that the police department must compensate witnesses for their testimony. How often does the police department have to pay witnesses?

On page 9, Section D, ID Technician Pearl compared latent prints collected. Have they been compared today? I believe she was trying to get to the truth in these cases.

In the report, page 13, Section IV, there are numerous similarities from the other victims to my attack, including:

• Kathleen D.—Knife near face, sex from behind, rob, rape, "do not look at me"

• Linda E.—Gun held while being forced to undress

• Deborah—Numerous cuts and stab wounds on neck and throat.

If Miller had documented my case and detailed the manner in which I was abducted, comparison would also have been made to the fact of our arms being held, Brown's hand on my collar, and about Deborah's neck too.

On pages 14-15, Section A, it states that several attempts at rape were made. Investigating officers should ask detailed questions to get the whole account, and not just bits and pieces. Penetration happened in the back seat, not outside of the car. I wondered if Miller was thinking about Kathleen D when he wrote the 2/5/1985 report in my absence. He had me read it and I let him know that it was incorrect. He said

159

he would change it to make it correct. He told me he was trying to help me. Obviously, the report should have been changed. Perhaps victims should be required to sign off on these corrections to make sure the crime reports are right.

On page 16, footnote 84 states that, when Willard Brown's picture was brought to Detective Crump from Detective Miller, it was like an unprepared sales presentation. From my perspective, both detectives talked 'over me' like I did not exist and they told me Brown was a suspect in another case, Deborah Sykes case. That is the reason why I thought all of the information had been compared in 1986. Again, it is obvious that these detectives were working on both cases at the same time.

On page 16, footnote 86, the document states that Detective Crump received my case because Bill Miller was promoted. Miller told me that Crump would contact me. On 8/24/2007, I confirmed this with Sergeant Mike Barker. He agreed this is what he remembered too.

From page 17, Paragraph 1, my question is how does the police department pass along police reports to the media and the public? Years ago, these reports were placed in a specific box for media access. I would like to know that this practice has changed, and that modern technology is being used to share police reports via email and scanning rather than the out-dated "box" method. This would help protect the future Linda E. and Kathleen D. cases from being shielded from the press.

I would also like to know how the police department searches for suspects today, and if the Uniform Division really did conduct a search for Willard Brown for ten months.

On page 17, the footnotes indicate that the SBI and the WSPD worked together in 1986 and 1989. I remember Detective Crump telling me that they were bringing all the victims, even the West End Blvd. victims (a white male rapist), to be interviewed. Who were the victims interviewed at that time? I also believe that the grey glove that Willard Brown wore during his crime against me would have contained skin cells that could be analyzed and compared using today's advanced DNA technology.

After reading pages 18 and 19, I have several unanswered questions. Was Gray pursued when Murphy identified him? Has the City of Winston-Salem responded to Mrs. Jefferson about the lost/missing evidence? Did they respond via letter, phone call, or personal visit?

As clarification on page 22, section XI, footnotes 119 Crump, Miller, Davida Martin (David Wagner's Daughter who was Brown's court-appointed attorney), one jail employee and I were all together present on the elevator when I identified Willard Brown from the line-up.

Moreover, on page 23, footnote 128 E, it should be noted that Detective Hicks also worked on Regina K's (the Integon Victim) case. Supplemental reports indicate that she and Miller visited other companies at 500 West 5th Street, which was the attack site of Linda E. and Regina K.

There appears to have been a vague and ineffectual process in place to keep track of files (page 24, footnote 133). In the insurance industry, we use file charge out cards when removing a file from a shelf for research. Detectives in 1985 could not tell me whether all of the pictures were present in the IDMO. How are pictures reviewed, removed, and returned today?

I would like to know when the police department was informed that my mother-in-law talked to Phoebe Zerwick and Mark Rabil. I would like to read Detective Rowe's 2004 Report of the interviews with Bill Miller and Carter Crump. These two individuals were responsible for investigating my case; yet there is compelling evidence that they deliberately covered-up the link between my case and the Sykes case.

I am aware that Vicki Pearl was treated in a similar manner to me, and that she was provided with quick, "no" responses to her questions and assertions.

On page 41, in section D, footnote 188 regarding the Willard Brown warrant, it is clear that our cases could have been, and should have been solved very early on in the investigations. Still, I was in and out of the police department until 1989 trying to get information and trying to get someone to help me.

I was told that when Brown was arrested, it was for suspicion in Deborah Sykes case, not in my case. If that is true, then why was my case further ignored? The cases were almost identical, with the one differing factor being that I was still alive.

Additional emphasis should also be placed on the handling of Linda E.'s case. Teresa Hicks was assigned to the case on June 15, 1984. But, on September 5, 1984, the rape kit and clothing evidence were destroyed. On September 8, 1984, the case was closed. Her case closed before she left town; yet, she was led to believe the opposite. This was during the same time frame that Darryl Hunt was arrested for the Deborah Sykes murder. Wouldn't it make sense to investigate these actions, especially since Teresa Hicks also investigated the other rape cases?

My last statement to Carter Crump in 1989 was, *"Wouldn't it be wild if one day we found out that the same person that killed Deborah was the same person that attacked me."* He responded that I should be glad I still had a life and could go on with my life.

Another baffling fact is that Crump contends he made a phone call and found out that Brown was in jail when Linda E. was attacked. There is no proof of this phone call; there is no documentation, there is no paperwork. Certainly, and logically, some effort should have been made to document this critical fact; however, there is no record whatsoever.

I was told by Detective Crump that he and I just had to believe what he was told about Willard Brown being in prison when Deborah was murdered. He could not give me anything in writing.

There are so many unanswered questions remaining. I am attaching a partial list as an appendix to this statement. The SARC report can be viewed and read in it's entirety at the following website:

http://www.cityofws.org/Home/Departments/MarketingAnd Communications/NewsArchive/News2007/Articles/CityAnn ouncesSettlement-Sykes-Hunt

I encourage everyone to read this shocking report. I do not believe that Willard Brown will ever be prosecuted for his crime against me. Moreover, I did not write my story in the hopes that he would be prosecuted. I am telling my story in hopes that the lessons contained therein will help hurting people and investigators.

Victory is mine! I found victory when the Lord saved my soul and saved me from eternal damnation. I found victory when God was there to save me from near death that day. I found victory when I am permitted to find healing in sharing this testimony. I found victory knowing the crime committed against me was used to bring clarity for the loved ones of Deborah Sykes and others. I found victory when Willard Brown went to prison for his crimes, I found victory in helping exonerate Darryl Hunt and his release from prison. I do not need to lose one moment of precious time wondering and worrying about Willard Brown, the police department, or anyone associated with what happened to me.

God knows. He brought me through this terrible ordeal so that I can help someone else who is suffering. That is God's plan; therefore, that is my purpose.

Regina K. Lane and Dr. Linda F. Felker

Questions

1. Daulton had to sign-off on my reports. Was he Detective Crump's supervisor at the time that I was deciding whether to prosecute Willard Brown? (Part 2) page 43 refers to #4)

2. Was Captain Gid Cornatzer Detective Miller's boss?

3. Sgt. Furman Mason was Daulton's supervisor. What was the hierarchy, the chain of command in the PD at that time? We know that orders come "top down." Was Daulton also Crump's supervisor? Where did Jerry Raker and others fit in this hierarchy?

4. When I rode the bus with Miller, Raker and Cornatzer were following in the car behind in case something came up. Why? Is this part of the hierarchy? What did they expect to happen? Is this common procedure?

5. I was told that Brown was arrested for Sykes case, not mine. The search warrant for the arrest cannot be located. How did Crump establish probable cause for the warrant to arrest Willard Brown? What was the real purpose of the warrant? My evidence was non-existent. To what was he going to compare – what evidence?

6. 2/5/85 report, Miller said Brown concluded his act. Was that what Crump was basing search warrant on? I had already told Crump that the rape did not happen outside the car.

7. Would a detective normally discuss similarities between cases, like Daulton, Miller, Crump?

8. At what point would these similarities be taken seriously enough to initiate re-investigation or research?

9. On pg 51 footnote 210, in addition to the Sykes/Kellar rapes, there is a comment that Brown a suspect in other rapes.

10. Whose rape was he suspected of? (Book page 51)

11. Why did the PD feel there was an information leak?

12. Where was the leak?

13. Who was involved, the DA to the media?

14. What was the purpose of this piece of information?

15. Was that the reason the file/evidence/investigation was on lockdown? Obviously, PD was under pressure to answer questions where no answers were available yet.

16. Why is there no documentation of the phone call to determine if Brown was in prison? There is no written evidence to substantiate Crump's claim that he made the call, to whom he spoke, etc.

17. What made the Sykes/Kellar cases different in the minds of the detectives?

18. With all the similarities laid out in front of them, they were working on these cases at the same time, what was it that kept them from drawing obviously conclusions about Brown?

19. Refer to pg 76 # 6. Victim, despite similarities, did not press charges. Why did PD try to make this appear that it was somehow my fault, even though they could not and did not assist me in solving my case?

20. After over a year of waiting for PD to pick up Brown, around 5/4/86, I was asked to make a final decision about prosecuting him; however, they had not submitted blood samples from Brown for ID at that time. What was the rush?

21. Why did they want my answer so quickly without having full information and the investigation complete?

22. Strange that the SBI did not draw any connection during their investigation. There is no documentation that the SBI ever asked any questions about the two cases. Dan Stone, SBI Agent, was in the car with Crump when Brown was arrested. What did they discuss about potential charges against Brown?

23. Dan Stone – What was his purpose in being in the car when Brown was arrested?

24. Dan Stone, and other SBI, were involved in research in both cases. Did they ask any questions or draw any conclusions about these cases being connected?

25. Isn't that part of their job?

26. Where is the documentation of communication between the SBI and PD on these questions/issues? *(Pg*

75...general questions # 1 talks about that. Both agents declined to be interviewed about this.)

27. Are the Sykes court transcripts available for public viewing?

28. What charges would have been brought against Willard Brown; should the attempted murder charge been added?

29. What time would have been served by Willard Brown if he had been convicted of the charges against me?

30. Would it have been more than 3-4 years, 5 years max?

31. On page 28, paragraph 2, the report states the Regina K.'s case involved kidnapping, rape and brutal assault. Why were the charges in my case so minimalized?

32. Why would I want to be represented by people who were unwilling to assist me?

33. Tom Keith said, *"The justice system is broken,"* and stated that our prisons are built in poor rural counties in order to provide work for people. My question is, "How are we going to fix our justice system?"

34. Detectives were not willing to send someone out to drink houses to ask questions. How far was the 1700 block of Claremont Avenue and 17th Street from 14th Street? That could have been where Brown became intoxicated before the attacks.

35. Was the composite drawing I made similar to or the same as Hooper's drawing for either attackers On page 32, item #6?

36. Was my case ever discussed with the District Attorney's office?

37. What was the upward channel of authority over Detectives Miller and Crump at that time? This would also apply to Raker, Cornantzer and Furman Mason.

38. Were Willard Brown and Thomas acquainted?

39. Were they in prison together at any time?

40. Did they violate another prisoner's rights?

41. Did Thomas live in High Point with Brown at any time?

42. How often does the police department have to pay

witnesses?

43. Technician Pearl compared latent prints collected. Have they been compared today?

44. Has the process used by the PD to pass police reports to the media and public changed? How does the police department pass along police reports to the media and the public how the police department searches for suspects today?

45. Did the Uniform Division really conduct a search for Willard Brown for ten months?

46. Was Gray pursued when Murphy identified him?

47. Has the City of Winston-Salem responded to Mrs. Jefferson about the lost/missing evidence?

48. Did they respond to her via letter, phone call, or personal visit?

49. How are pictures reviewed, removed, and returned today?

50. When did Phoebe Zerwick and Mark Rabil let police department know about my mother-in-law's call to them about Willard Brown?

51. What kind of written changes could I request of the State and Forsyth Correctional Center so they will keep more accurate records of release of prisoners?

52. Where was the Police Department to media leak?

53. Whose fingerprints were on Deborah's car?

About the Authors

Regina K. Lane

Regina Lane lives life close to her family, where she and Scott, her husband of 26 years, have raised their sons Michael and Stephen. They are blessed with two beautiful daughters-in-law, Samantha and Whitney.

Regina still works in the PMI insurance industry with many of her friends from 27 years ago. She considers this a testimony of God's work in her life as she prayed and believed that God would do something awesome.

Regina desires to be an encouragement and inspiration to those around her as she continues to share her testimony at various group meetings around the Triad. She sang with the Faith Harmony Quartet since 1999 and sings with Grace Harmony and The Sounds of Grace musical groups, extensions of her home church, and Grace Baptist Temple Choir.

Her 2006 interview can be seen on HBO's *The Trials of Darryl Hunt*, where her story is a special featurette. She was a guest of WUNC Radio on the *State of Things*. Most recently, she was interviewed with Cineflix for Discovery Channel's *Cold Blood 4* for 2012. This episode is called "Her Own Way".

Dr. Linda F. Felker

D r. Linda F. Felker is the Owner and President of Felker Consulting, Inc. She provides professional development analysis, leadership training, authoring, career guidance, and counseling. She holds a charter certification to administer the Myers Briggs Type Indicator and conducts couples, individual, and group sessions on psychological and personality type in relationships.

Linda is a frequent guest speaker at Leadership and Women's Conferences across the country, and is a published author of many books, including *Lessons From the Purple Tree, Homewreckers, Giggles in the Garden,* and *Ladies of Grace.*

Linda and her husband David have three children and two grandchildren. She is a charter member of Grace Baptist Temple in Winston-Salem, N. C., where she sings in the Adult Choir and assists with the Grace Notes Children's Choir.

www.ingramcontent.com/pod-product-compliance
Lightning Source LLC
LaVergne TN
LVHW051736080426
835511LV00018B/3087